D0481256

Modern First Ladies

Their Documentary Legacy

Modern First Ladies

Their Documentary Legacy

COMPILED AND EDITED BY
NANCY KEGAN SMITH
AND
MARY C. RYAN

INTRODUCTION AND AFTERWORD BY
LEWIS L. GOULD
University of Texas

FOREWORD BY
DON W. WILSON
Archivist of the United States

NATIONAL ARCHIVES AND RECORDS ADMINISTRATION
WASHINGTON, D.C.

PUBLISHED FOR THE
NATIONAL ARCHIVES AND RECORDS ADMINISTRATION
BY THE NATIONAL ARCHIVES TRUST FUND BOARD
1989

Library of Congress Cataloging-in-Publication Data

Modern first ladies.

1. Presidents—United States—Wives—Archives.
I. Smith, Nancy Kegan. II. Ryan, Mary C., 1960–
CD3029.82M63 1988 973.9'092'2 88-15263
ISBN 0-911333-73-8

Designed by Serene Feldman Werblood, National Archives
Composed in Goudy Old Style by Harper Graphics, Inc.,
Waldorf, Maryland
Printed by Walsworth Press, Marceline, Missouri.

Picture Credits: cover: Nancy Davis Reagan, courtesy of The White House; Eleanor Roosevelt, credit Bachrach, Inc.; Lady Bird Johnson, courtesy of the Lyndon B. Johnson Library. P. 1, Douglas Chandor, *Eleanor Roosevelt* (detail), 1949, courtesy White House Historical Association; pp. 4, 97, 105, 170, John F. Kennedy Library; pp. 5, 47, 51, 53, 56, Herbert Hoover Library; pp. 7, 83, 86, 89, 91, 168, Dwight D. Eisenhower Library; pp. 10, 59, 62, 65, 67, Franklin D. Roosevelt Library; pp. 13, 131, 134, 137, 140, 173, Gerald R. Ford Library; pp. 19, 28, 33, 38, Library of Congress; p. 56, credit Bettmann Newsphotos; pp. 71, 75, 76, 80, Harry S. Truman Library; p. 101, courtesy CBS News; pp. 109, 112, 115, 118, Lyndon B. Johnson Library; pp. 121, 124, 127, 129, Nixon Presidential Materials Staff; pp. 143, 147, 150, 151, Jimmy Carter Library; pp. 155, 158, 161, 163, The White House.

Table of Contents

Foreword

The wives of the presidents of the United States have begun to emerge recently as subjects for serious scholarly investigation on their own merits. A number of factors have led to this increased attention to the role and position of the first lady. Nancy Reagan's fame and her visibility as a force in her husband's administration, coupled with her advocacy of measures to curb drug abuse, have focused public concern on what the wife of a president may properly do. The rise of women's history has led researchers to consider the contributions of such figures as Lucy Webb Hayes, Mary Todd Lincoln, and Edith Roosevelt to the tradition of first ladies. Students of the presidency have also begun to realize that the men who have held the nation's highest office were husbands, fathers, and individuals with complex, emotional lives. Leaving their wives out of what presidents did produced an incomplete record, and presidential scholars have moved, sometimes very slowly, to address this issue.

The growth of presidential libraries during the 1970s and 1980s has been a positive force in providing a rich body of source material regarding what modern first ladies have done. In some instances, the Social Files in these repositories contain thousands of boxes of documents and letters that disclose how individual first ladies functioned and how the American public responded to their work. For years, society has regarded first ladies as models of what women should be and how they should act. As separate collections, the Social Files are important sources for discovering how women were perceived in the United States in this century. As a collective resource, the files dramatically expand the range of primary documentation.

An exploration of the records of first ladies will no doubt elicit diverse insights about the historical impact of these women on their times. Interpretive theories that explain modern first ladies are still tentative and exploratory. All scholars in this new field recognize the central place of Eleanor Roosevelt as an activist model for the presidential wives who followed her, but despite the shelves of books on Mrs. Roosevelt, many phases of her own rich life have yet to be fully investigated. The contributions of her twentieth-century predecessors also need to be more intensively examined. The first ladies who immediately followed Eleanor Roosevelt reacted to her example by stressing their own individual styles. Bess Truman, Mamie Eisenhower, and Jacqueline Kennedy made a point of saying that they were *not* Mrs. Roosevelt. Lady Bird Johnson built upon Mrs.

Roosevelt's example during her environmental campaigns. The accomplishments of Pat Nixon, Betty Ford, and Rosalynn Carter will be tracked and discussed in light of the activist model as writers look at the sources about them in the presidential libraries.

Some general propositions have emerged as possible ways of understanding the increased attention paid to first ladies. Their role as a partner of the president has often been suggested as a key to their popular influence with American citizens. An alternative argument is that their arrival into the public spotlight has been a function of the overall rise of the power of women in national life. Since first ladies are a form of political celebrity, it is credible to regard their fame as one way that society comes to terms with women who have visible influence in areas where men have usually dominated. None of these explanations have yet been tested in a systematic way because the whole field remains in a formative and preliminary stage. That is why the availability of so much fresh documentary evidence in the Social Files of these women represents exciting opportunities for analysis and debate about modern first ladies.

Whatever direction historical writing on presidential wives may follow, there is little question that the future role of first ladies is more likely to expand than to recede to the days of relatively silent and passive helpmates. By the end of this century, the wives of presidents are likely to be women with their own professional careers and substantial reputations that parallel their husbands' achievements. Beyond the probable expansion of the duties of the first lady lies the uncharted territory of what will happen when the election of the first woman president raises the question of the role and responsibilities of "the first gentleman of the land."

When that fundamental shift occurs, the institution of the first lady in the form the nation has known it since the days of Martha Washington will pass from the scene. For now, the first lady remains one of the most fascinating and unexplored facets of the American presidency and the history of women in the United States. Nancy Reagan has said that the first lady has "a white glove pulpit" from which she can reach out to her fellow citizens. The many ways that presidential wives have attempted to fulfill the demanding, rewarding, and frustrating imperatives of their position are outlined well in this volume. In 1929 Mary Roberts Rinehart wrote that "the public interest in the lives and duties of our First Ladies is equaled only by the general ignorance of their lives and a misapprehension of their duties and special privileges." This book is an endeavor to show what presidential libraries can offer to the interested scholar and writer, as well as the public in general, in an effort to penetrate what Rinehart called "the veil of mystery" that has surrounded women who have added much to the record of American history in this century.

Don W. Wilson
Archivist of the United States

Modern First Ladies
An Institutional Perspective

By *Lewis L. Gould*

Detail from Douglas Chandor's portrait of Eleanor Roosevelt at age 65. Courtesy White House Historical Association.

The first lady, because she is the wife of the chief executive, occupies one of the most watched and evaluated positions associated with the American presidency. She has, however, no formal or legal standing in the national government. In 1968 the administration of Lyndon B. Johnson considered issuing an executive order to accord a more permanent status to the First Lady's Committee for a More Beautiful Capital that Lady Bird Johnson had set up in 1965 to beautify Washington, D.C.[1] A presidential aide reported that one argument weighing against the proposal was that "the First Lady has never been given official duties by law or executive order, and this would be a break with tradition." For that and other reasons, the order was not issued. Though the role of the first lady has expanded since 1968, the uncertain institutional status of the president's wife has persisted down to the present day.[2]

Even the title "First Lady" arouses some negative responses. Jacqueline Kennedy did not like the term, and Arthur M. Schlesinger, then a presidential staff member, agreed. "As an anti-monarchist," he told Pierre Salinger in June 1961, "I would consider 'Mrs. John F. Kennedy' far more appropriate."[3] More important, there is no consensus on how to characterize the role of the president's wife. She does not occupy an official position or rank, she receives no salary, and she has an intangible, imprecise, but significant influence on the president. The first lady is an institution in American government that is as important as it is ill-defined.

During the past decade, scholarship on presidential wives has begun to emerge as a self-conscious field of study. Biographies of individual women, especially Eleanor Roosevelt, have appeared, and several general treatments of all or some of the first ladies are in progress or nearing completion.[4] Doctoral dissertations are also under way on various aspects of what first ladies do or how the public sees them.[5] Two initial explanations offered for the importance of presidential wives are their standing as representatives of American women and their status as political celebrities. No doubt other interpretations will emerge as the field develops.[6]

Historical writing on first ladies has not, for the most part, had either a comparative sense of how one wife's activities related to her predecessors in the White House or a substantial body of primary sources that would allow for sustained research into what first ladies have achieved. The institution of the

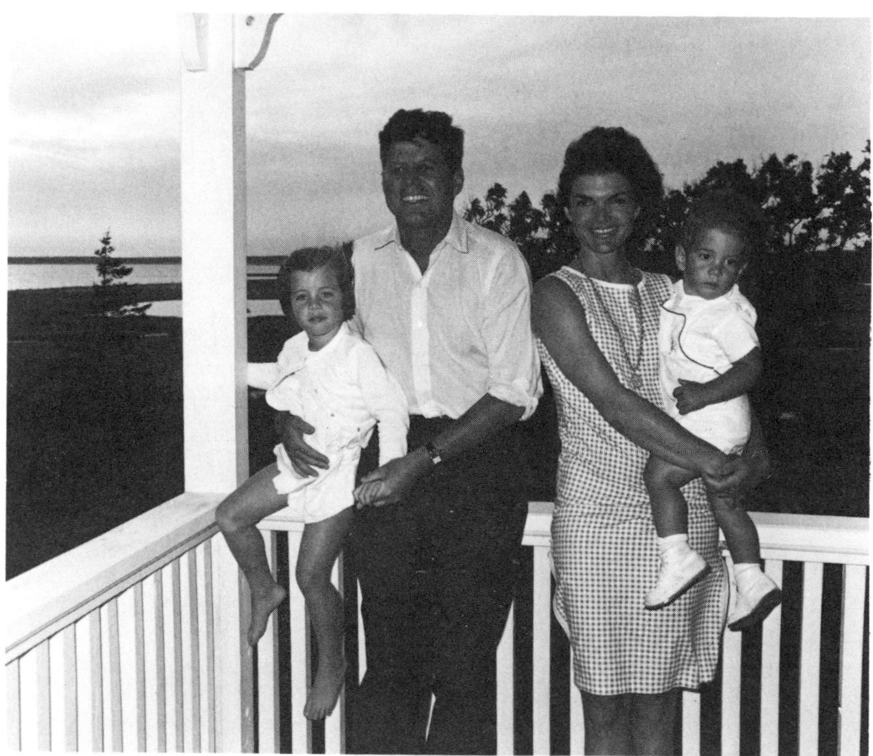

The Kennedys brought the first young children into the White House since the days of Theodore Roosevelt. Mrs. Kennedy was only 31 on Inauguration Day, 1961.

first lady has lacked an institutional history. As the presidential libraries have begun reviewing and opening the White House Social Files and the personal papers for the wife of each modern president, a rich lode of information has come to light. The following collection of essays indicates how much students of the presidency, of American women, and of the subjects that have engaged the first ladies will find in the abundant holdings of the presidential libraries.

In a brief summary essay it is not possible to cover all phases of first ladies in this century. Rather the history of the institution itself, and the contributions of some of the women who have sustained the first ladies, merit attention. When Edith Kermit Roosevelt came to the White House in September 1901, there was nothing that could be construed as the staff for the first lady. Under President James A. Garfield, an Office of Social Correspondence, or Social Bureau, had been created to deal with the mail that related to White House guests and the transmission of official invitations to formal occasions. The actual business of the social relations was the responsibility of the assistant secretary to the president. For first ladies themselves, relatives or friends were the most common sources of help to meet the demands of the position.[7]

Eighty-five years later there is now an "Office of the First Lady" for Nancy Reagan with a chief of staff, a press secretary, a director of projects, and a bureaucracy of several dozen people that parallels the one that serves the president. How did the evolution of the first lady's staff proceed in this century, and who were the major women figures in the development of the modern structure of the institution? This essay will trace how the expansion of the support structure for first ladies occurred.

Edith Kermit Roosevelt took the initial step toward an institutional base for presidential wives when she employed Isabella "Belle" Hagner of Washington, D.C., as the first social secretary in 1902. Mrs. Roosevelt had ambitions to make the presidency and the White House the social arbiter of the nation's capital, and that goal required more formal assistance than female relatives could provide.[8] Hagner was one of the District's emerging cadre of "social secretaries" to local society families and had worked in the War Department for the family of Secretary Russell A. Alger in 1898–99. Mrs. Roosevelt learned of Hagner's abilities and brought her into the White House once the mansion was renovated in 1902. The social secretary appeared on the White House payroll as a clerk at a salary of $1400 a year. Hagner assisted the first lady with the steady round of musicales, receptions, and teas that marked Mrs. Roosevelt's years in Washington. She "really is the chief factor at the White House," wrote presidential military aide Archie Butt in June 1908. "She went there merely as the social secretary of Mrs. Roosevelt, but her sphere has broadened until it is sort of head aide, general manager, and superintendent." The tall and ample Hagner reg-

Posing on a pack mule at Acton, California, in 1891, sixteen-year-old Lou Henry grew up to become a fine horsewoman; she remained an avid hiker and camper into her mid-sixties.

ularly briefed Washington's women society reporters and was generally an adept player of the social game, as several military officers who crossed her found out.[9]

Under the Roosevelts, Belle Hagner became a Washington celebrity. Her visibility did not suit Helen Herron Taft, who wanted to minimize connections with the Roosevelt White House. Hagner was not retained as social secretary and became a clerk in the State Department. "Mrs. Taft frankly declared she wished a clerk not a companion." Her first social secretary, Alice Blech, came over from the Bureau of American Republics and stayed for a year, until her marriage. Unlike Hagner, she filled in the society journalists over the phone about Mrs. Taft's schedule. The second social secretary, Mary D. Spiers, was recruited from the surgeon general's office but lasted only a few weeks with the demanding and ailing Mrs. Taft. In the last two years of her husband's presidency, Helen Taft relied on her daughter and other relatives for assistance in her social duties.[10]

The election of Woodrow Wilson in 1912 brought Belle Hagner back to the White House as social secretary to Ellen Axson Wilson. Mrs. Wilson's personal secretary was a relative, Helen Bones, but she and the three Wilson daughters looked to Hagner for advice about social engagements and the various activities that Mrs. Wilson pursued. Hagner's tenure lasted past Mrs. Wilson's death in August 1914 until her engagement to Norman James at the end of 1915. She established a continuity of service and a practice of dealing with the public that became a model for the social secretaries who followed her.[11]

Hagner's successor, Edith Benham, was another Washington social secretary who had worked for Sen. Winthrop Murray Crane of Massachusetts and for the Russian embassy. She spent five years in the White House before her marriage to Adm. James M. Helm in 1920. The First World War, the Paris Peace Conference (which Helm attended with the Wilsons), and the president's serious illness in 1919–20 restricted the social secretary's duties between 1917 and 1921. While serving at a canteen with Edith Wilson during the war, she got to know Eleanor Roosevelt. Helm developed the techniques and routine of the social secretary in these years that she would use again a decade later.

Florence Kling Harding also drew on the pool of Washington social secretaries for her own social secretary, Laura Harlan. Mrs. Harding's interest in Republican politics, women's affairs, and the prevention of cruelty to animals evoked enough mail that it became necessary for Harlan to have a regular assistant social secretary, Coranelle Mattern. By this time the work of the Social Bureau was becoming more elaborate and complex. One part of its staff handled the invitations and lists that related to White House entertaining. The correspondence section, directed by a White House stenographer, Ralph Magee, preserved and filed the mail from the public that increasingly flowed to the first lady. Form letters had been devised to deal with the plethora of requests for her to issue statements, intervene with government agencies, and make personal appearances. The role of the first lady was beginning to achieve a permanent and institutionalized status.[13]

After the death of Warren G. Harding in August 1923 brought Calvin Coolidge to the presidency, Grace Coolidge employed a new social secretary, Mary Randolph, who stayed on until 1930. Randolph's memoirs reflected the expanded burdens of the social secretary. "The job of being White House Sec-

The Heart Fund held special meaning for Mrs. Eisenhower, whose husband suffered a heart attack in 1955. Susan Kasper opens the 10th annual campaign as noted heart specialist Dr. Paul D. White looks on.

retary, charged with seeing that appearances, at any rate, are always proper, is a strenuous, grueling job—a twenty-four hour job." Relations with the press formed an increasing part of the social secretary's assignment. Society editors in Washington were now allowed to view the settings for White House dinners in advance of the occasion and regularly received information about guests and general aspects of the program. Mrs. Coolidge did not give interviews or make statements, but the emphasis of the social secretary's position was more and more in the direction of how it affected the first lady's public image.[14]

Although she was a more activist presidential wife between 1929 and 1933 than scholars have realized, Lou Henry Hoover did not enhance or enlarge the role of the social secretary. Mrs. Hoover used her three personal secretaries on behalf of her favorite causes such as the Girl Scouts. Mary Randolph was the social secretary for the first year of the Hoover administration and then resigned in June 1930. Reports of a difference of opinion with the demanding Mrs. Hoover over table decorations for a dinner and an announcement to the press accompanied Randolph's departure. The first lady then turned to a series of friends and secretaries from outside Washington to perform the duties of the position. "The girls from the great open spaces," wrote Frances Parkinson Keyes, "had been catapulted into positions for which they were handicapped by their inexperience."[15] To the degree that Lou Henry Hoover fell short of her goals as first lady, it owed much to her failure to follow the established practices, exemplified in the social secretary, of how Washington expected a presidential wife to function.

Making an impression on Washington and the nation was never a problem for Eleanor Roosevelt between 1933 and 1945, but she showed a greater sensitivity to the opinions of social circles in the capital than had Mrs. Hoover. In addition to her personal secretary, Malvina "Tommy" Thompson, Mrs. Roosevelt asked Edith Helm to return as her social secretary. In so doing, Eleanor Roosevelt recognized that she had to accommodate the social demands of her position sufficiently to prevent Washington gossip from undermining the other causes she wished to pursue.[16]

The invitations that Eleanor Roosevelt issued to the public to write her with their questions and problems, the lecturing and touring that she did, and the political activities in which she engaged produced such an unprecedented outpouring of mail that the Social Bureau had to borrow additional personnel to deal with the flow. The first lady's innovation of regular press conferences with the female reporters gave her a kind of *de facto* press office to publicize the issues that moved her. The journalists did not have an adversarial relationship with her, and they served as conduits and collaborators for the news the first lady wished to see in print. By her later years in Washington this mutually beneficial connection had been solidified in the White House Press Conference Association.[17]

In place of a large personal staff, however, Eleanor Roosevelt drew on her network of friends, confidants, and hangers-on, some of whom lived at the White House at various times. These recruits from her entourage included the former reporter, Lorena Hickok, her young protégé, Joseph Lash, and her first biographer, Ruby Black. Others came and went as the first lady's needs required. Like the contributions of Mrs. Roosevelt herself, these personal aides were more pervasive than focused, but they did enable the first lady to pursue her diverse and ever-shifting agenda of good works. They also suggested that future first ladies might need a larger supporting staff structure if they wished to be as active as Eleanor Roosevelt had been.[18]

Bess Truman's White House years represented a reaction to the style of Eleanor Roosevelt. The practice of regular press conferences ended immediately, and Mrs. Truman was as terse as her predecessor had been voluble. Some important continuities remained. Edith Helm stayed on as social secretary, and her duties now expanded to include conducting regular weekly press briefings with the first lady's personal secretary, Reathel Odum. Later in the Truman presidency, Odum relinquished these duties entirely to Helm. The social secretary then decided that it would be simpler to give journalists a copy of Mrs. Truman's list of social engagements along with the name of the hostess or sponsoring group. "I believe Mrs. Truman was the first wife of a President ever to have such a mimeographed record of her comings and goings." Like so many other efforts to meet public interest in the first lady, this innovation was continued for Mrs. Truman's successors.[19]

During the Truman years the White House was renovated while the president and the first lady lived in Blair House. Congress created the Commission on the Renovation of the Executive Mansion, a body that anticipated other commissions and committees, formal and informal, that would assist the first lady in the management and appearance of the White House and later in the pursuit of favored projects. The role of the Trumans was advisory, and Mrs. Truman had no specific or direct connection with the commission as such. Her years in the post of first lady demonstrated, however, that even the most passive presidential wife would need more staff help and have more connections with the press than had been the case before Eleanor Roosevelt.[20]

Mamie Eisenhower endeavored to get along without a real social secretary during her husband's two terms. She told the press in the spring of 1953 that she intended to name a social secretary, but at the end of the year the White House announced that Mrs. Eisenhower's personal secretary, Mary Jane McCaffree, would handle those duties as well. It was not a successful experiment. When her uncertain health permitted, Mrs. Eisenhower wanted to pursue an active schedule on her own terms, and there were some minor flaps when she and her staff tried to escape from the rigors of receiving lines and long occasions. "The social and physical strains imposed on the wife of the President steadily are increasing," the press noted, but the first lady tried to operate in the style of Mrs. Taft or Mrs. Hoover with about as much staff assistance.[21] In 1960 McCaffree admitted to Letitia Baldrige, the incoming social secretary for Jacqueline Kennedy, that the White House "can't handle Mrs. Eisenhower's mail properly. They are snowed under and have no proper direction and, as a result, the letters they prepare aren't first rate." It was becoming evident that future first ladies would need a larger bureaucratic support structure to deal with the increased public curiosity regarding the occupants of the position.[22]

In addition to the selection of Baldrige, who had experience in private business, as her social secretary, Jacqueline Kennedy took an important new step in the evolution of the first lady when she named Pamela Turnure as her assistant social secretary for the press. The aim of what Mrs. Kennedy did was as much to control what the press knew about her activities as first lady as it was to facilitate coverage. "I don't think a First Lady should have a Press Secretary," Kennedy wrote, and she told Turnure to "invent some ladylike little title for yourself." Whatever the motives behind Turnure's selection, it indicated that a first lady could no longer combine the duties of the social secretary and representative to the press corps in a single person. The social and entertaining side of the White House expanded relentlessly, as did the extent of journalistic attention to the first lady, when television network news focused on the president and his family.[23]

To help carry on her work of renovating and restoring the White House,

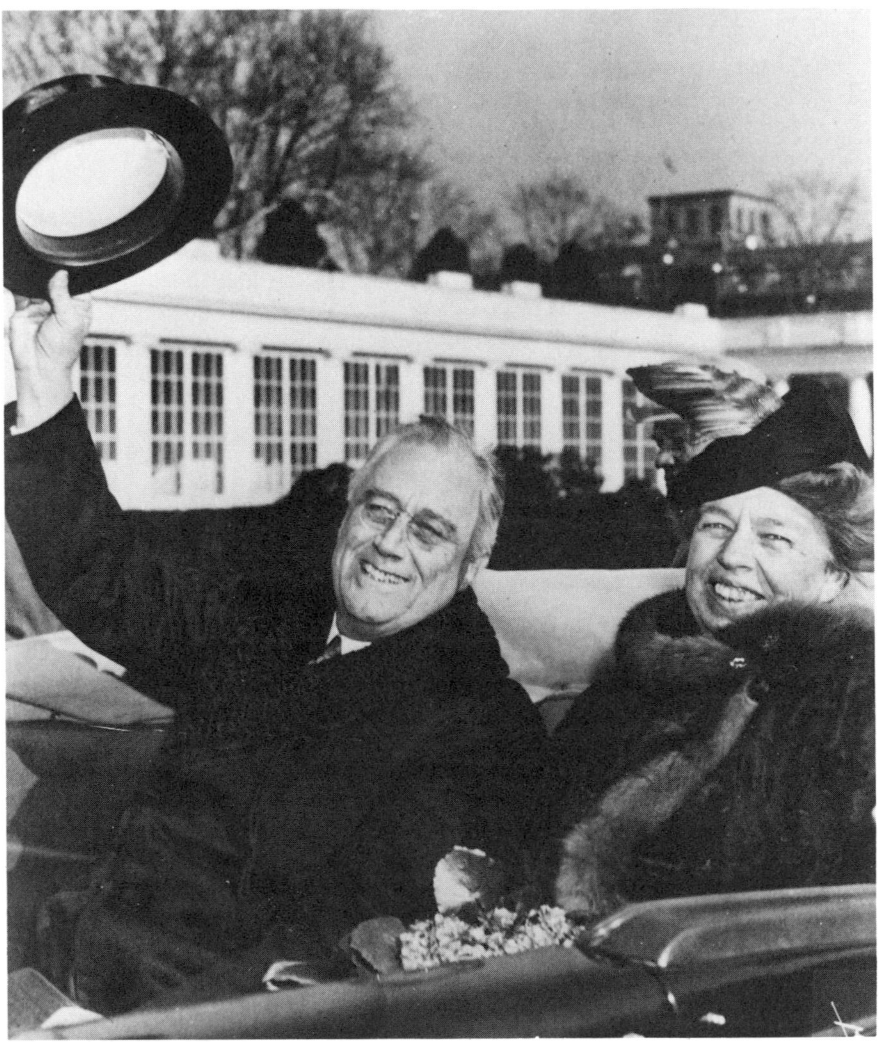

Not one to sit quietly in the back seat, Eleanor Roosevelt set the standard for active first ladies.

Mrs. Kennedy used a variety of informal committees and panels including the Fine Arts Committee for the White House, established in late February 1961. She also encouraged the creation of the White House Historical Association that same year and asked Congress to enact legislation giving the National Park Service authority over the historic features of the Executive Mansion. The first lady also employed a curator for the White House, first Lorraine Pearce, then William Elder, and ultimately James Ketchum. President Lyndon Johnson made the post of curator official in March 1964 in an executive order to set up the Committee for the Preservation of the White House. Mrs. Kennedy's actions helped to put in place a continuing structure of programs and positions that would provide other first ladies with the means to pursue their own priorities as presidential wives.[24]

Lady Bird Johnson's appointment of Elizabeth S. "Liz" Carpenter as staff director and press secretary in 1963 marked as decisive a change in the history of the institution as Edith Roosevelt's selection of Belle Hagner as social secretary in 1902. Johnson also named a social secretary, the talented and knowledgeable Bess Abell, but it was Carpenter who became the visible link between the first lady, the press, and the public. Her title also indicated that the wife of a president would have a staff because she needed one. After her husband defeated Barry Goldwater in 1964, Lady Bird Johnson chose beautification of the environment as her principal cause, and she and Carpenter embarked on campaigns to change the appearance of Washington, D.C., control outdoor advertising, and raise popular awareness of the nation's beauty. Liz Carpenter served both the first lady and the president, and she was never timid about letting men in the White House know what she thought.[25]

To carry out the beautification program, Lady Bird Johnson recruited a program-oriented staff. From the Department of the Interior she brought over Sharon Francis as staff assistant for beautification to act as public liaison with environmental groups, the bureaucracy, and Capitol Hill. Within the White House Cynthia Wilson emerged as the aide who functioned as an all-purpose "inside" implementer, writing press releases, doing advance work on trips, and monitoring the incoming beautification correspondence. Mrs. Johnson also had an assistant, Simone Poulain, who coordinated her television appearances.[26]

Along with the people who worked directly for her, Lady Bird Johnson followed the example of Eleanor Roosevelt and Jacqueline Kennedy and reached out to a diverse array of private citizens through her First Lady's Committee for a More Beautiful Capital and its private offshoot, the Society for a More Beautiful National Capital. In this way such benefactors as Brooke Astor, Mary Lasker, and Laurance Rockefeller worked in tandem with Walter Washington, a black leader in the District, Polly Shackleton, a Democratic activist in Washington, and landscape architect Lawrence Halprin. During the four years between 1965 and 1969, Lady Bird Johnson showed how creatively a first lady could draw upon the staff resources and volunteer assistance that her position naturally attracted.[27]

Though the degree of first lady involvement and participation fluctuated in the succeeding two decades after Lady Bird Johnson left Washington, the pattern of a press secretary and a social secretary handling the divergent demands on the time of a president's wife endured. During Pat Nixon's years in the White House, a formal administrative structure replaced the *ad hoc* arrangements that Mrs. Johnson had used. Constance Stuart served as Mrs. Nixon's staff director and, between 1969 and 1973, coordinated the five offices that assisted the first lady. In addition to the offices of the Social Secretary and Press Relations, there were the Administrative, Appointments/Scheduling, and Correspondence offices. Relations between Mrs. Nixon's operation and the West Wing of the White House were always uneasy. After Stuart left in 1973, and with the Watergate crisis growing, the first lady became her own staff director through early August 1974.[28]

Betty Ford's relatively brief tenure as first lady brought additional refinements and specialization to the White House operation for the president's wife. There were now a deputy press secretary, an assistant press secretary for press advance work, and an appointments secretary to deal with Mrs. Ford's demanding public schedule. The first lady had an officially designated speechwriter as well. In all, twenty-eight staff members worked in Mrs. Ford's office as she pursued such causes as the ratification of the Equal Rights Amendment in a visible way. She wished "to be remembered for being able to communicate with people," and to that end she employed the substantial bureaucratic apparatus that supported her in the White House.[29]

Rosalynn Carter came to the presidency intending to be as activist a first lady as Eleanor Roosevelt and Lady Bird Johnson had been. She acted as her own chief of staff, and her press secretary, Mary Finch Hoyt, was also called "East Wing Coordinator." The organizational categories of the staff resembled those that Pat Nixon had used but reflected Mrs. Carter's own priorities—Social Affairs, Press and Research, Projects and Community Liaison, and Scheduling and Advance. With the first lady's strong interest in mental health, the Equal Rights Amendment, and the general record of her husband's administration, the staff of more than twenty people had a demanding agenda between 1977 and 1981.[30]

The organization of the two dozen people who performed similar functions for Nancy Reagan in the 1980s showed the effect of the expansion of the first lady's institutional base. The letters that Mrs. Reagan's aides sent out came from the "Office of the First Lady," and press releases spoke of the "Office of the First Lady's Press Secretary." The social secretary had her own "deputy secretary," and there were the familiar chief of staff, projects director, and the assistants who did the advance work on Mrs. Reagan's trips. As Nancy Reagan's antidrug campaign burgeoned in the mid-1980s, a need emerged for additional personnel to handle conferences and media events that dominated the effort to persuade everyone to "just say no."[31]

The transformation from Belle Hagner working alone in the Roosevelt White House to an elaborate apparatus in the East Wing that resembles a miniature presidency dramatically underscores the evolution of the institution of the first lady. Americans expect the wife of a president to be more than a hostess and passive helpmate. "I discovered I would find it difficult to just sit here and not do anything except entertain," Nancy Reagan said in late 1984. "For me, having a goal is important."[32] The choice was not entirely Nancy Reagan's to make. Because of the contributions of Eleanor Roosevelt, Lady Bird Johnson, Betty Ford, and Rosalynn Carter, the activist model for first ladies seems firmly in place. Mrs. Reagan's causes were conservative, but the means by which she followed them built on the example and techniques of her predecessors. In the future, historians, political scientists, and students of the presidency in general will look more intensively at what first ladies have done since 1900. As they do, they will find that close attention to the role of the social secretaries, the press secretaries, and the modern staff members who sustain a president's wife offers an important and informative perspective on how the institution of the first lady has paralleled the growth of the modern presidency itself.

At home with her husband, Betty Ford takes time to relax. She believed that the country was ready for a first lady with a mind of her own and the courage to speak it.

NOTES

[1]Matthew Nimetz to Joseph Califano, July 31, 1968, Beautification, box 257, Office Files of James Gaither, Lyndon Baines Johnson Library, Austin, TX. For information on the First Lady's Committee for a More Beautiful Capital, see Lewis L. Gould, "Lady Bird Johnson and Beautification," in Robert A. Divine, ed., *The Johnson Years, Volume Two* (1987).

[2]Joseph Califano to Lady Bird Johnson, Sept. 30, 1968, Natural Resources, July 1, 1968—, box 6, White House Central Files, LBJ Library. Mrs. Johnson did not wish to be seen as trying to bind Mrs. Richard M. Nixon about what should be done as first lady. Interview of Sharon Francis, oral history, June 27, 1969, pp. 66–67 of transcript, LBJ Library.

[3]Arthur M. Schlesinger, Jr., to Pierre Salinger, June 2, 1961, "Jacqueline Kennedy, 1961," box 705, White House Central Subject File (WHCSF), John F. Kennedy Library, Boston, MA. See also Arthur M. Schlesinger, Jr., *A Thousand Days: John F. Kennedy in the White House* (1965), p. 669.

[4]The following books are not meant to be an exhaustive list but rather to indicate the range of scholarship that is being pursued in the field. Among recent biographies are Emily Apt Geer, *First Lady: The Life of Lucy Webb Hayes* (1984); Frances Wright Saunders, *Ellen Axson Wilson: First Lady Between Two*

Worlds (1985); Margaret Truman, *Bess W. Truman* (1986); Julie Nixon Eisenhower, *Pat Nixon: The Untold Story* (1986); J. William Youngs, *Eleanor Roosevelt: A Personal and Public Life* (1985); and Joan Hoff-Wilson and Marjorie Lightman, eds., *Without Precedent: The Life and Career of Eleanor Roosevelt* (1984). A forthcoming overview of all the women who have been first lady is Betty Boyd Caroli, *First Ladies* (1987).

[5]Barbara Oney Garvey, "A Rhetorical-Humanistic Analysis of the Relationship Between First Ladies and the Way Women Find a Place in Society" (Ph.D. diss., Ohio State University, 1978); Myra Greenberg Gutin, "The President's Partner: The First Lady as Public Communicator, 1920–1976" (Ph.D. diss., University of Michigan, 1983).

[6]Lewis L. Gould, "First Ladies," *The American Scholar* 55(Autumn 1986): 528–535, treats these women as political celebrities.

[7]Edith Benham Helm, *The Captains and the Kings* (1954), p. 154, mentions the origins of the Social Bureau. For the way the White House handled social matters before 1902, see C. C. Buel, "Our Fellow Citizen of the White House: The Official Cares of a President of the United States," *Century Magazine* 53(1897): 652. For a newspaper report that a woman named Alice Sanger functioned as a social secretary in the administration of Benjamin Harrison, working directly for the president's secretary, Elijah W. Halford, see "Mrs. Taft's New Secretary—Miss Mary D. Spiers," *New York Times*, Mar. 13, 1910.

[8]On Edith Roosevelt's ambitions, see Abby G. Baker, "Social Duties of Mrs. Roosevelt," *Pearson's Magazine* 10 (Dec. 1903): 523–532, and Lawrence F. Abbott, ed., *The Letters of Archie Butt, Personal Aid to President Roosevelt* (1924), pp. 30, 126–127. See also Sylvia Jukes Morris, *Edith Kermit Roosevelt: Portrait of a First Lady* (1980), pp. 226, 227, 235–237.

[9]"Mrs. James Aided Presidential Wives," *New York Times*, Nov. 2, 1943; Abbott, ed., *Letters of Archie Butt*, p. 53; George B. Cortelyou to Edward Bok, July 2, 1902, author's collection. There are Belle Hagner letters to and from the Roosevelt family in the Peter Hagner Papers, Southern Historical Collection, University of North Carolina, Chapel Hill, NC. For more on Hagner, see *New York Herald Tribune*, Oct. 30, 1932, and Jonathan Daniels, *Washington Quadrille: The Dance Beside the Documents* (1968), p. 63.

[10]Abbott, ed., *Letters of Archie Butt*, p. 206; the quotation is from "Mrs. Taft's New Secretary—Miss Mary D. Spiers," *New York Times*, Mar. 13, 1910; for Alice Blech, see Fred W. Carpenter, "Memorandum For Miss Blech," Nov. 12, 1909, series 5, case file 3924; and for Spiers, Mary Dandridge Spiers to William Howard Taft, Apr. 15, 1910, series 5, case file 3567, Papers of William Howard Taft, Manuscript Division, Library of Congress; Ishbel Ross, *An American Family: The*

Tafts, 1678 to 1964 (1964), pp. 243, 264; "Changes at the White House," *New York Times*, Mar. 4, 1909; Mrs. William Howard Taft, *Recollections of Full Years* (1914).

[11]"Mrs. Wilson's Secretary," *New York Times*, Dec. 25, 1912, announced Hagner's return. Her duties are outlined in Helen Woodrow Bones to Jessie Woodrow Bones Brower, Feb. 23, 1913, in Arthur S. Link et al., eds., *The Papers of Woodrow Wilson*, vol. 29, *1913–1914* (1979), p. 555; Walter P. Webb and Terrell Webb, eds., *Washington Wife: Journal of Ellen Maury Slayden from 1897 to 1919* (1963), pp. 200, 203; *New York Times*, Oct. 25, 1915; *Washington Post*, Nov. 2, 1943.

[12]Helm, *Captains and the Kings*, pp. 46–125, covers her years in the Wilson White House. She published excerpts from her diaries of this period in the book. The originals are in the Edith Benham Helm Papers, Manuscript Div., LC; fuller portions of the diary have also been published in Arthur S. Link et al., eds., *The Papers of Woodrow Wilson*, vol. 53, *1918–1919* (1986), pp. 319–321, 343–344, passim.

[13]Laura Harlan to the Girl Scouts of Atlanta, Oct. 21, 1921, Coranelle Mattern to Florence Kling Harding, Mar. 8, 1922, Laura Harlan to Allen F. Moore, June 21, 1922, Laura Harlan to Florence Kling Harding, July 27, 1922, Florence Kling Harding Papers, roll 242, Papers of Warren G. Harding, Ohio Historical Society, Columbus (microfilm). Harlan was the daughter of Supreme Court Justice John Marshall Harlan. Daniels, *Washington Quadrille*, p. 101.

[14]Mary Randolph, *Presidents and First Ladies* (1936), p. 5. Randolph's book is one of the most perceptive and informative written by a social secretary. On her role in the White House, see Edward T. Clark to F. C. Hicks, Oct. 31, 1925, Edward T. Clark to Mary Randolph, Nov. 10, 1928, series 1, file 3290, Papers of Calvin Coolidge, Manuscript Div., LC. Ishbel Ross, *Grace Coolidge and Her Era: The Story of a President's Wife* (1962), pp. 97, 98, 99, 144, 145.

[15]Frances Parkinson Keyes, *Capital Kaleidoscope: The Story of a Washington Hostess* (1937), p. 185. Keyes is more candid than Randolph, who gives a sense of the difficulties of working for Mrs. Hoover but does not talk about what caused her to leave the White House in *Presidents and First Ladies*, pp. 117–155. On Mrs. Hoover's problems in securing a replacement for Mary Randolph and the brief career of Helen Greene, see "Mrs. Hoover Still Lacks a Social Secretary; Capital Wonders if She Will Act for Herself," *New York Times*, Oct. 3, 1930; and "Miss Ruth Fesler Honored," *New York Times*, May 12, 1931, about her private secretary who also served as social secretary. Helen B. Pryor, *Lou Henry Hoover: Gallant First Lady* (1969) is the only biography of Mrs. Hoover to date.

[16]Helm, *Captains and the Kings*, pp. 135–152. For an example of what Helm did for Eleanor Roosevelt, see Edith B. Helm to Anna J. Pennybacker, Jan. 10, 1934, Anna J. Pen-

nybacker Papers, Eugene C. Barker Texas History Center, University of Texas at Austin. I am indebted to Stacy Rozek for this reference.

[17]Maurine Beasley, "Eleanor Roosevelt's Press Conferences: Symbolic Importance of a Pseudo-Event," *Journalism Quarterly*, 61(Summer 1984): 274–279; Maurine Beasley and Paul Belgrade, "Eleanor Roosevelt: First Lady as Radio Pioneer," *Journalism History* 11(Autumn–Winter 1984): 42–45. For the White House Press Conference Association, see its "Rules," Dec. 1944, Newswomen-Buffet, box 28, White House Social Office Files, Harry S. Truman Library, Independence, MO. Maurine Beasley's forthcoming book on Eleanor Roosevelt and the press will discuss these issues in thorough and fascinating detail. On the borrowing of federal employees to work in the White House, see Ruth K. McClure, ed., *Eleanor Roosevelt, An Eager Spirit: The Letters of Dorothy Dow, 1933–1945* (1984), pp. 17–39.

[18]The best place to begin for Eleanor Roosevelt's friendships is Joseph P. Lash, *Love Eleanor: Eleanor Roosevelt and Her Friends* (1982), Doris Faber, *The Life of Lorena Hickok: E. R.'s Friend* (1980), and Ruby A. Black, *Eleanor Roosevelt: A Biography* (1940). Also useful on Eleanor Roosevelt's career in the White House is James R. Kearney, *Anna Eleanor Roosevelt: The Evolution of a Reformer* (1968).

[19]Helm, *Captains and the Kings*, p. 286; Margaret Truman, *Bess W. Truman*, pp. 256–257, 260–261, touches on matters relating to her mother's staff. The social files and other records at the Truman Library are illuminating on Mrs. Truman's personal style. See Charles G. Ross to Edith B. Helm, Dec. 21, 1949, box 34, President's Personal File, Aug.–Dec. 1949; William F. McCandless to George Harvey, Feb. 2, 1950, box 34, President's Personal File, Jan.–June 1950; and "Mrs. Truman's Engagements to be given to the Press, April 29, 1952," Press Meetings, 1949–1952, box 17, White House Social Office Files, HST Library. For more on Mrs. Truman's decision not to hold press conferences, see Ruth Montgomery to "Dear Fellow Members," June 8, 1945, Bess Furman Papers, Ms.Div., LC.

[20]Edwin Bateman Morris, comp., *Report of the Commission on the Renovation of the Executive Mansion* (1952); Margaret Truman, *Bess W. Truman*, pp. 336–338, 340–341.

[21] "First Lady at Work," *Newsweek*, Feb. 16, 1953, p. 27; "First Lady Drops Social Aide Plan," *New York Times*, Oct. 1, 1953; "Why Mamie 'Takes It Easy,' " *U.S. News & World Report*, May 13, 1955, pp. 46, 49; Mrs. Eisenhower's social office records are available for research at the Dwight D. Eisenhower Library, Abilene, KS.

[22]Letitia Baldridge is quoted in Mary Van Rensselaer Thayer, *Jacqueline Kennedy: The White House Years* (1971), p. 17.

[23]Thayer, *Jacqueline Kennedy*, pp. 33, 34; on Mrs. Kennedy's press relations, see Pamela Turnure, "Memorandum For the President," Feb. 26, 1962, "Jacqueline Kennedy, Jan. 1, 1962–Mar. 10, 1962," box 705, WHCSF; Pamela Turnure to Pierre Salinger, Oct. 12, 1962, "Jacqueline Kennedy, May 1, 1962–Dec. 10, 1962," box 705, WHCSF, JFK Library.

[24]Thayer, *Jacqueline Kennedy*, pp. 281–337. Lorraine Pearce to Leon C. Baldwin, May 29, 1961, author's collection; Letitia Baldrige to Kenneth C. O'Donnell, July 25, 1961, "White House 3," box 1005, WHCSF; Pierre Salinger, "Memorandum for The Record," May 25, 1962, "White House 3–1, Acquisitions," box 1006, WHCSF, JFK Library, indicate some of the sources that are available on Mrs. Kennedy pending the opening of her social office files.

[25]Liz Carpenter, *Ruffles and Flourishes* (1970), is her own engaging and informative memoir of her White House service. Carpenter published another book of reflections and reminiscences in 1987. Her oral history interviews in the Johnson Library are extensive and enlightening, and much of her working correspondence can be found in the Liz Carpenter Subject Files and the Liz Carpenter Alphabetical Files, White House Social Files (WHSF), LBJ Library. For more on Carpenter's activities, see Gould, "Lady Bird Johnson and Beautification," in Divine, ed., *The Johnson Years, Volume Two*, and Gould, "First Lady as Catalyst: Lady Bird Johnson and Highway Beautification in the 1960s," *Environmental Review* 10(Summer 1986): 77–92.

[26]For Sharon Francis, see her oral history, May 20, 1969, pp. 8–10 of transcript, LBJ Library; Gould interview of Cynthia Wilson, done for the Johnson Library, to be included with their oral history project. In addition to the materials already cited on Lady Bird Johnson, see the article by Nancy Kegan Smith in this issue.

[27]*Beautification Summary: The Committee for a More Beautiful Capital, 1965–1968*, prepared for Mrs. Johnson in 1968 and which is in the Johnson Library, is the best introduction to the work of her committee. See also Mary Lasker to Lady Bird Johnson, July 22, 1965, "Suggestions of D.C. Projects," box 8, Beautification Files, White House Social Files; Polly Shackleton to Laurance Rockefeller, July 18, 1967, "Project Trailblazers," box 8, Beautification Files, WHSF; Sharon Francis to Walter Washington, Nov. 21, 1966, "Capper Plaza," box 5, Beautification Files, WHSF; Lawrence Halprin to Polly Shackleton, Apr. 25, 1967, "Capital East-Inner Blocks," box 5, Beautification Files, WHSF; Lady Bird Johnson to Brooke Astor, May 24, 1965, "Beautification-Special," box 15, Liz Carpenter Alphabetical File, WHSF, all LBJ Library.

[28]In addition to the essay on Pat Nixon in this volume, the most helpful single source is Julie Nixon Eisenhower, *Pat Nixon: The Untold Story* (1986). The Watergate episode also

brought out a few items relating to the first lady and her staff. See, for example, Constance Stuart to Mrs. Nixon, Feb. 15, 1971, in U.S., House of Representatives, *Examination of President Nixon's Tax Returns For 1969 through 1972*. 93d Cong., 2d sess. Report No. 93-966 (1974), p. A-598. Also see Constance Stuart to Bob Haldeman, Aug. 11, 1970, in Helen Thomas, *Dateline: White House* (1975), pp. 167–169.

[29]On Betty Ford, see Susan Porter to Mrs. Frederick Brisson, Aug. 13, 1976, for the work of the appointments secretary, author's collection; Sheila Rabb Weidenfeld, *First Lady's Lady: With the Fords at the White House* (1979), pp. 69, 75, gives a sense of how Mrs. Ford's office worked, but must be used with caution. Mrs. Ford has written two memoirs: Betty Ford with Chris Chase, *The Times of My Life* (1978), and Betty Ford with Chris Chase, *A Glad Awakening* (1987). The latter volume is more candid about Mrs. Ford's alcoholism. For the quotation from Mrs. Ford, see "Woman of the Year," *Newsweek*, Dec. 29, 1975, p. 21.

[30]The essay on Mrs. Carter's paper in this book indicates the range of her concerns as first lady. She discusses how she organized the White House staff in Rosalynn Carter, *First Lady From Plains* (1984), pp. 168–176. Mary Finch Hoyt to Lewis L. Gould, Jan. 19, 1987, and Feb. 17, 1987, provided very helpful information.

[31]Biographies of Nancy Reagan have already begun to appear. Frances Spatz Leighton, *The Search for the Real Nancy Reagan* (1987), pp. 276–277, 334, mentions some of the staff arrangements in passing. For indications of how Mrs. Reagan's staff met her needs, see Sheryl Eberly, deputy director of correspondence, Office of the First Lady, to David Phillips, May 7, 1981, copy in author's collection, courtesy of Mr. Phillips; "The Foster Grandparent Program—Dear to the Heart of Nancy Reagan," The White House, Office of the First Lady's Press Secretary, Nov. 10, 1981; and "Summary of Mrs. Reagan's Activities Against Drug and Alcohol Abuse," Office of the First Lady's Press Secretary, author's collection. On the organization of her staff, "Co-Starring at The White House," *Time*, Jan. 14, 1985, p. 30.

[32]"A Talk With Nancy Reagan," *Time*, Jan. 14, 1985, p. 31.

Meeting a New Century

The Papers of Four Twentieth-Century First Ladies

By Mary M. Wolfskill

Theodore Roosevelt's second wife, Edith Kermit Carow (1861–1948), and their five children: Quentin, Kermit, Archibald (with dog), Theodore, and Ethel. A private woman, Mrs. Roosevelt maintained a long and dedicated interest in providing clothing to the poor.

The Manuscript Division of the Library of Congress houses papers of twenty-three presidents ranging from George Washington to Calvin Coolidge. In some of these collections there is not a single document of a first lady. For the twentieth century, documentation increases as we move from the administrations of Theodore Roosevelt (1901–1909) to William Howard Taft (1909–13) to Woodrow Wilson (1913–21); however, not one item by or to Grace Coolidge can be found in the Library's collection of her husband's papers. It should be noted that the papers of Florence Harding comprise a series within the collection of her husband, Warren G. Harding, which is in the custody of the Ohio Historical Society.

The papers of the early twentieth-century first ladies are relatively few compared to those of their successors, who have large collections apart from those of their husbands. Edith Roosevelt destroyed many of her papers. Helen Taft suffered a stroke shortly after the inauguration and wrote very little during her tenure as first lady. Ellen Wilson died after only seventeen months in the White House, and World War I and a gravely ill husband prevented Edith Wilson from assuming the traditional round of social activities associated with her office. In each of these cases, papers illuminating the lives and work of these first ladies are interfiled with those of their husbands. Edith Wilson alone has a separate collection of papers; the bulk of this collection, however, begins after her husband's death in 1924. In addition, many of the letters of these first ladies were handwritten, and there appears to have been little effort to retain copies other than for repetitive routine responses.

Despite the limitations, one can use the presidential papers to understand the changing role of the twentieth-century first ladies, the ways in which their individual personalities shaped that role, and the ways in which they were perceived by the American public. Born between 1860 and 1872, Edith Roosevelt, Helen Taft, and Ellen and Edith Wilson shared a common Victorian-era upbringing. They carried many of the values that characterized that age into their role as first lady. For traditional upper- and middle-class women, that meant a commitment to the primacy of family life and privacy. During a time when mass-circulation newspapers and human-interest journals were becoming increasingly popular vehicles of information, these women kept a low profile, rarely granting personal interviews. They avoided any identification with the "new woman" who sought political equality and campaigned for woman suffrage. By examining the lives and documentary heritage of Edith Roosevelt, Helen Taft, Ellen Wilson, and Edith Wilson during their years in the White House, we can gain some insight about the ways in which they influenced their husbands' careers, the ways they affected important social and political decisions and finally, how the role of the first lady evolved and changed during the early twentieth century.

I

Born in 1861 in Norwich, Connecticut, into a family of comfortable financial means, Edith Kermit Carow Roosevelt appears to have been brought up to be a first lady. Her forebears could claim an American lineage dating back to the 1630s, having descended from the well-known theologian Jonathan Edwards.[1] Among her closest friends were the Roosevelts, with whom she shared part of her early education and often joined for vacations at the Roosevelt family summer home at Oyster Bay, Long Island. Although she attended the Comstock School in New York City, much of her education came from her cultural surroundings. There is some evidence that Theodore Roosevelt and Edith Carow talked of marriage when she was in her late teens and he was beginning his studies at Harvard.

In his junior year, however, Roosevelt fell in love with Alice Hathaway Lee, and they were married two years later. Tragedy was to befall this brief but happy union, and in his diary for February 14, 1884, Theodore Roosevelt wrote, "The light has gone out of my life."[2] On that day his wife of little more than three years died after giving birth to a baby girl, Alice (later Mrs. Nicholas Longworth). There was a double tragedy on that day, for Roosevelt's mother also had died in the same house only a few hours earlier.

Nineteen months later, Edith Carow and Theodore Roosevelt renewed their close friendship, and in December of 1886 they were married in London, England. Over the next ten years, Edith Roosevelt gave birth to five children: Theodore (1887), Kermit (1889), Ethel (1891), Archibald (1894), and Quentin (1897). When the family entered the White House in 1901, the children, including Alice, ranged in age from four to seventeen.

Edith Roosevelt was a profoundly private person who believed that a lady's name should appear in the newspapers only three times in her life—at birth, marriage, and death. This sense of privacy has contributed to the difficulty biographers have had in attempting to present an accurate and detailed picture of her life. She was also a realist, however, and recognized that the intrusion of the press into the daily life of the White House would be inevitable.[3] Following the death of her husband, Edith Roosevelt involved herself in many activities that would memorialize his work, including the publication of his writings.[4]

She became concerned, however, about the possible future publication of his letters to her, which she felt to be an invasion of privacy, and began destroying personal files. She was familiar with the works of Elizabeth and Robert Browning and considered "the exposure of their intimate thoughts" as "horribly distasteful." She told a friend, "I could not bear the idea that this could happen to me."[5] In addition, there is evidence that Edith Roosevelt instructed executive office staff to discard correspondence. On one letter she noted, "I have answered this so destroy it. E"[6]

Although many of Edith Roosevelt's papers no longer exist, there are approximately twenty-four hundred items of correspondence dating from 1891 to 1919 in the Theodore Roosevelt Papers in the Library of Congress as well as newspaper articles about her in the scrapbook series for the years 1895 to 1909. Most of the correspondence is interfiled in a group of incoming letters in Series I of the papers and in volumes 105, 106, and 107 of the letterpress copybooks in Series II. These latter volumes are devoted almost exclusively to responses by Mrs. Roosevelt or those written on her behalf by her private secretary, Isabelle (Belle) Hagner, and by various secretaries to the president, including George B. Cortelyou and William Loeb.

Most of the incoming letters do not appear to have survived, but it is not too difficult to discern the types of requests made upon the first lady from the more or less standard responses given, such as:

> While many of the cases brought to Mrs. Roosevelt's attention appeal to her sympathies and excite her cordial interest, she has made it a rule not to take any part in Government affairs, the necessity for which practice will upon reflection be apparent to you.[7]

Often the responses indicate to the writer that his or her request had been forwarded for action to the appropriate government official or agency, such as the Commissioner of Pensions, Secretary of the Navy or War, Civil Service Commission, or Attorney General. Much of the correspondence consists of Mrs. Roosevelt's polite rejections of numerous gifts, invitations, and dedications of books and musical scores, as well as solicitations addressed to her for money, photographs, items for fairs, autographs, and memberships in organizations.

Just as her husband had created an administrative framework that would relieve him of the overwhelming paperwork of the office by giving much of the work to subordinates, Edith Roosevelt hired a private secretary to deal with the voluminous daily correspondence of the first lady. According to her biographer Sylvia Jukes Morris, the appointment of Isabelle Hagner was "one of the most successful innovations Edith made."[8]

Hagner had all the qualifications for the job. She was tactful, diplomatic, and knowledgeable about Washington society. She seemed to fit perfectly into the Roosevelt household, where she came to be thought of as the "oldest child in that big, affectionate family, and the Roosevelts leaned on her in all the crises of their long years in the White House."[9] Archibald Butt, military aide to the president, said of Miss Hagner, "she is the chief factor at the White House, and the fact that everything has gone as smoothly as it has is due more to her than everyone else put together about the Executive Mansion."[10] "Belle Hagner's keen eye was everywhere," wrote another observer.[11] She helped maintain the privacy that Edith Roosevelt so greatly enjoyed. Avoiding personal interviews, and rarely meeting with reporters, Mrs. Roosevelt decided what information was to be published and left it to Belle to release it to journalists who were in "good standing."[12]

One of the first actions the Roosevelts undertook was to remodel the White House and add a wing at the side to house the president's staff. The addition created a greater separation between the sphere of the president and that of the first lady. Speaking of the newly reconstructed White House complex, one journalist noted that "No official or other visitor may cross its threshold without an intimation that the attention is desired. The steady stream of visitors to the new, separate White House offices can turn only longing, curious eyes over to the front door of the President's house."[13] The president's own sisters were required to make appointments to visit. Along with this renovation, Edith Roosevelt created a special gallery to display the portraits of the first ladies. As one visitor commented, "It seems to me it has rescued those admirable females from oblivion."[14] She also supervised the inventory and expansion of the White House china collection to provide for the greater number of people who could now be seated comfortably at large state dinners.

Mrs. Roosevelt kept a schedule for recurring social events, such as teas with the wives of cabinet members; allowed time for exercise; and put aside a portion of each day for the children. She found it difficult to let go of her growing family and, in reserving a place for Ethel as a boarder at the National Cathedral School, told the headmistress, "She is still so young that I cannot bear to part with her entirely." Arrangements were made for her daughter to return to the White House for the weekends.[15] While she was loving, she was also straightforward when her children misbehaved. She wrote to Kermit about a school report, "I am rather disappointed in your report, because even if you could not have done better in your languages you could surely have avoided all those fifteen black marks or the greater portion of them."[16]

She was also capable of voicing her dissatisfaction to others who had not lived up to her expectations. When the seamstress of her second inaugural gown provided a description of it to a newspaper before the event, she vented her feelings. "Greatly annoyed by your advertisement of my gown in New York Sun," she telegrammed. "No such thing is done by tailor here or by any tradespeople serving the White House. Fear this makes it impossible for me to employ you again."[17] When a piece of mail miscarried because of a slight omission on the envelope, she instructed a secretary to inform the postmaster that

> Mrs. Roosevelt has suggested that your attention be called to the accompanying envelope. It appears that the communication was mailed in this city April 13th, sent to the *State* of Washington, and delivered at the White House in the mail this noon. Mrs. Roosevelt thinks the omission of D.C. should not have sent it so far astray.[18]

Especially noteworthy is Edith's involvement in communications with highly placed diplomats. This is evidenced by letters from Whitelaw Reid and Cecil Spring-Rice. Reid had been appointed ambassador to England by Theodore Roosevelt. In this capacity he sent regular communiques, usually only a few pages in length, to the president reporting on matters of state. To Mrs. Roosevelt, however, he sent long letters, sometimes numbering over twenty typed pages, describing in great detail his adventures with English society, political intrigues, and the course of events on the European continent.

As the letters include descriptions of "shooting" outings as well as elegant dinners, they were most likely intended for both the president and his wife, and appear to be, in part, an attempt to justify the large sums of government funds supporting Reid's diplomatic post. The Reids lived in great splendor in England, and one writer commented that "the ambassador seemed quite in place amid the sumptuous furnishings . . . and that he had a simple and sincere love of grandeur."[19]

Others, however, were more critical, and Reid complained to Mrs. Roosevelt, "I am a good deal disgusted at some recent examples of enormous exaggeration and falsification going on in the Democratic press at home about my houses and expenses here."[20] In 1910 Edith Roosevelt was the guest of the ambassador in England and later wrote that "no one really knew Mr. Reid who did not see him in his own house . . . in London." In describing him she commented that he "typified whimsical American charm."[21]

Reid's observations provide valuable insight into the British political and social happenings of the day. Reflections on Winston Churchill are both entertaining and enlightening. Reid wrote to the first lady that Sir Henry Campbell-Bannerman, one of Churchill's colleagues in Parliament, spoke of Churchill "as having grown distinctly on the House as to ability;—he did not add as to prudence!" This same colleague, Reid continued, indicated that he feared Churchill "was destined to a brief career, and that it was probably his own knowledge of this which led him to such vehement efforts to go as far as he could in the time left him."[22] In another letter to Mrs. Roosevelt, Reid noted that Churchill was very unpopular, even hated "for his bad manners, his recklessness and the row he has stirred up in South Africa."[23]

British diplomat Cecil Spring-Rice served as best man at the Roosevelts' wedding in 1886 and remained a close friend. Edith Roosevelt was especially fond of him, and early in Roosevelt's presidency she wrote to him revealing her thoughts on the role of women and her feeling about being first lady. "It was good to hear from you and it will be even better to see you," she wrote:

> Last night the Lodges and Mr. Adams and Austin Wadsworth and his wife were here and we talked of you and of the empty place which you have left. I count on long misty moonlight evenings on the White House porch, Theodore in his rocking chair, you and Cabot settling world affairs over your cigars, while Mrs. Lodge and I meekly listen as becomes our sex and position. Being the centre of things is very interesting, yet the same proportions remain. When I read "The World is too much with us" or "Oh for a closer walk with God" they mean just what they did, so I don't believe I have been forced into the "first lady of the land" model of my predecessors.[24]

The president attempted to have Spring-Rice assigned to the British embassy in Washington, but such a prestigious post went only to more senior British statesmen. He was, instead, assigned to Russia, where his intimate knowledge and keen observation of political maneuvering in the struggle between Russia and Japan over Manchuria provided Theodore Roosevelt with the intelligence he needed to act as negotiator between these two powers.

Because of his junior position in the British foreign service, Spring-Rice needed to keep his communications secret from both the U.S. State Department and the British Embassy. This prompted him to write to Mrs. Roosevelt to avoid inspection of his correspondence. In December 1903 Spring-Rice informed the first lady that "the feeling here is that no one but Russia has a right to be in

Asia; it is the natural destiny of the Russian people to live supreme and solitary in Asia."[25]

Meanwhile, internal conflicts and revolution were brewing in the country, and in March of 1905 he tried to describe to Mrs. Roosevelt the chaotic conditions during the Russian revolution:

> . . . anarchy is growing and incidents abound. It would be difficult to give an idea of the disintegration which is taking place. It is like a great animal dead and rotting, with jackals tugging at its tough hide. The peasants are going round in bands destroying and sometimes killing . . . The Ministers themselves are resigning every day—and the Tsar won't accept their resignations. The centre of Government and source of power is hidden in his palace surrounded by his soldiers and spies—and no one can get at him to tell him the truth.[26]

Not only Cecil Spring-Rice, but also American novelist Owen Wister and historian Henry Adams were counted among Edith Roosevelt's many admirers who were impressed with her intellectual abilities and gracious manner. Owen Wister once wrote to Theodore Roosevelt, "Please tell Mrs. Roosevelt I shall bring her a new French Play—hoping she's not read it. She reads everything before I do."[27] Henry Adams proclaimed, "Would the President have a ghost of a chance if Mrs. Roosevelt ran against him?"[28]

The newspapers described her as "a model of wifely and motherly devotion."[29] Jacob Riis, close Roosevelt family friend, noted that the companionship of her husband and children were the "chief end of her life," and to this end, as biographer Sylvia Jukes Morris observes, she was the "archetypal Victorian patrician lady" who truly found her role as wife and mother fulfilling.[30] On the occasion of her eightieth birthday on August 6, 1941, an editorial in *The New York Times* proclaimed Edith Roosevelt "a great as well as a beloved woman," recalling her "well-stored mind," "gracious presence and nature," and "kindness as well as dignity" that characterized her years as first lady.[31]

II

As his presidency drew to a close, Theodore Roosevelt selected William Howard Taft to succeed him. The Republican party and the American people supported his choice, and in March of 1909 Taft began what was to become a very trying and unhappy four years in office. Few first ladies, however, were more enthusiastic about taking on their duties than Helen Herron Taft. She was far more ambitious to occupy the White House than her husband, who found "American politics" to be "most distasteful."[32] During Roosevelt's administration, Taft was twice offered a place on the Supreme Court, which he coveted, but Nellie (as Mrs. Taft was called) persuaded him to decline these offers, since they would not bring him closer to the presidency. She even went so far as to meet with Roosevelt to discuss her husband's political future.

Following Taft's inauguration, the new first lady decided to break with precedent and ride back with her husband from the Capitol to the White House. Traditionally, the outgoing president would assume this role, but Roosevelt had already made plans to go directly to the railway station following the ceremony. In her memoir, Nellie Taft wrote that "for me that drive was the proudest and happiest event of Inauguration Day. Perhaps I had a little secret elation in thinking that I was doing something which no woman had ever done before." She also remembered, however, that "some of the members of the Inaugural Committee expressed their disapproval, but I had my way and in spite of protests took my place at my husband's side."[33]

Helen Herron Taft was born in Cincinnati in 1861, into what she described as a "large family on moderate income."[34] The fourth of eleven children, eight of whom survived infancy, Nellie was known to be independent and ambitious, and even considered somewhat bohemian for her day.[35] An excellent student at Miss Nourse's private school in Cincinnati, she had a special interest in reading and particularly in music, which in her early years was "the inspiration of all . . . dreams and ambitions."[36] After graduation she taught school for several years. Her father, John Williamson Herron, was a lawyer who took an active interest in Republican party politics in Ohio, counting among his friends Benjamin Harrison and Rutherford B. Hayes, and shared a law practice for a time with Hayes. As a teenager, the future first lady enjoyed a week at the White House as the guest of Lucy Hayes and later recalled that this was "a very important event" in her life.[37]

Nellie Herron first met William Howard Taft when she was eighteen and they shared a bobsled ride at a coasting party. Later he joined with other young friends at a Saturday night "Salon" organized by Miss Herron to discuss literary works and to put on amateur theater productions.[38] It was through these meetings that Taft's appreciation of Nellie grew. He was impressed by her scholarly interests, industriousness, independence, teaching experience, and thirst for knowledge.[39] He also seemed to have an inkling of her ambition. "I hope you will think of me tomorrow when you take your Sunday afternoon walk along the beautiful streets of Washington," he wrote to her before their marriage in June 1886. "I wonder, Nellie dear, if you and I will ever be there in any official capacity. Oh yes, I forgot, of course we shall when you become Secretary of the Treasury."[40]

Looking back on her years in the White House, Mrs. Taft recalled that her active participation in her "husband's career came to an end when he became President." "I had always had the satisfaction of knowing almost as much as he about the politics and the intricacies of any situation in which he found himself," she wrote, "and my life was filled with interests of a most unusual kind. But in the White House I found my own duties too engrossing to permit me to follow him long or very far into the governmental maze which soon enveloped him."[41]

She did not, however, completely divorce herself from her husband's work. Shortly after Taft assumed the presidency he sent his wife the following message:

> March 25, 1909
>
> Memorandum for Mrs. Taft—the real President from the nominal President:
>
> If you are going to give Gist Blair a place in this Administration you had better talk with the Attorney General about him. He has the power of appointment over in his Department. Don't come to me, who have very little influence in this Administration.[42]

Nellie Taft's influence in her husband's administration was well known, and some observers, such as Henry Cabot Lodge, objected. White House usher Irwin (Ike) Hoover "pictured Mrs. Taft as continually projecting herself into

official discussions and joining her husband when she saw him deep in conversation with important politicians."[43] It was obvious to insiders that she helped make the decisions about who would be given diplomatic posts and who would not. Henry White's loss of his ambassadorial post in France was credited to Mrs. Taft, and the president's reluctance to appoint Nicholas Longworth as minister to China was attributed to Mrs. Taft's disapproval of Alice Roosevelt Longworth.[44]

Like Edith Roosevelt, Helen Taft engaged the services of a private secretary, Alice Blech, to assist her with the elaborate dinner parties and other social functions. Better versed in music than any previous first lady, she held sophisticated musicales, which often featured scores by Verdi, Strauss, Gounod, Bizet, and Mascagni.[45]

Her papers, scattered among those of her husband, document these activities as well as her earlier and later life. Among the more than 125 items that date from before her marriage are two diaries. In the earlier one, which begins in September 1879, Nellie Herron confesses to feelings of "fear and trembling" about her "coming out."[46] There are over one hundred letters from William Howard Taft written during their courtship, although few of Nellie's letters from this period appear to have survived. Later items include Nellie Taft's diaries written during her honeymoon trip, a trip to Europe, and a trip around the world, and four volumes of diaries documenting her White House years. The index to the Taft papers lists approximately 4,400 items in her name located in thirteen of the twenty-six series of material that comprise the papers. In addition, information about her can be found in other series. For the presidential years there are approximately 635 index entries, but researchers should also look at the "Professional Diaries" in Series 10, which describe social events and activities that included Mrs. Taft.

Nellie Taft's great elation on the realization of her dream to be the mistress of the White House was short lived. On May 17, 1909, she suffered a severe stroke that affected her face and speech. Few people were aware of the extent of her illness, and she eventually recovered, although she retained a slight speech impediment. President Taft found the situation very difficult. In May 1910 he confessed to Theodore Roosevelt that Nellie was "not an easy patient and any attempt to control her only increased the nervous strain." On a slightly encouraging note, Taft later wrote, "Gradually she has gained strength and she has taken part in receptions where she could speak a formula greeting, but dinners and social reunions where she has had to talk she has avoided."[47]

In 1910 Alice Blech left the position of private secretary to get married, and her replacement, Mary Dandridge Spiers, who came to the White House from a secretarial post in the Surgeon General's office, was dismissed after only sixteen days. Apparently, Spiers and Mrs. Taft were incompatible; Spiers also felt that she was inadequately compensated. Spiers had been told in a previous

Helen Herron Taft (1861–1943). Mrs. Taft was a brilliant woman and the driving force behind her husband's political fortunes. The capital's famous Japanese cherry trees surrounding the Tidal Basin were planted at her request.

position that "no woman would be promoted to a higher salary than . . . $1400.00," and she was hoping that a position in the White House would eventually lead to advancement. She was clearly disappointed with Mrs. Taft's desire "to make a change" and protested to the president, "I regret that I have not been able to be of some real service to Mrs. Taft but my stay has been so brief, I could scarcely have proven myself valuable."[48]

No secretary was hired to replace Miss Spiers, and Mrs. Taft's sisters took turns spending time with her and assisting with White House functions. Mrs. Taft was fairly quickly able to resume directing social activities from her upstairs room, although she was clearly frustrated by her ill health. She wrote to her husband, "I do not like this thing of being silent, but I don't know what to do about it."[49] Nellie was still very much interested in her husband's work. During state dinners she would often dine alone in an adjoining room where, unobserved, she could hear the music and dinner conversation.[50]

She received many letters requesting that she be an intermediary from people who were fearful that their correspondence, if sent through direct channels to the president, would never reach him. One writer requested her to ask her husband to "shake the Political Tree" so that "one of the Plums" would fall his way.[51] Most often, however, the letters were from women writing as "one mother to another," "for the sake of American Womanhood," or because they felt that she belonged "to the people."[52]

In most cases Mrs. Taft directed the letters to the proper authorities for an investigation of the particulars in each matter. For example, a woman claiming some familiarity with the first lady from her work at the Booklovers Library requested that Mrs. Taft intercede on behalf of her sister who wished a position in the government service.[53] Although the Civil Service Commission reported that an Executive Order could not be recommended in this case, a member of the Executive Office staff wrote a note to the president saying that "This is a case in which Mrs. Taft is interested and . . . in view of Mrs. Taft's interest the President may wish to issue one."[54]

Mrs. Taft also interceded on behalf of a small child who was refused admittance to this country by the immigration officials because he was believed to be an "idiot." Less than a week after Mrs. Taft received a letter from the mother of the child explaining that her son was "merely badly tongue-tied," the decision was reversed with the ruling that the case was "one of unusual hardship" and adding that "the family has Mrs. Taft to thank for the decision."[55]

In another incident, a woman supporting the establishment of kindergartens for black children in the South asked to speak with Mrs. Taft and the president about her plans. Mrs. Taft directed her secretary to set up the appointment.[56] And a newspaper proclaimed, "President Heeds Mrs. Taft's Plea for Mercy for Condemned Man." The article that followed stated that the president was not inclined to "interfere with the carrying out of the death penalty until Mrs. Taft intervened." The sentence was commuted to life imprisonment.[57]

Mrs. Taft was criticized for her lack of commitment to temperance. She believed that people should decide the issue for themselves. Since it was well known that William Howard Taft abstained from the use of alcohol, supporters of prohibition made a plea for the "banishment of intoxicants from the White House table." They claimed that "a great majority of . . . most thoughtful progressive people would welcome and applaud" this move and that it was "in harmony with the altruistic spirit of the times."[58] Mrs. Taft was not persuaded, and on one letter concerning this issue she instructed her secretary, Miss Blech, not to answer and noted at the bottom of the letter, "I think when they ask the President's attitude on temperance matters, we send what he said in some Yale lectures on local option etc.—but it is useless to say anything in cases like the above."[59]

Some of the most interesting correspondence to Mrs. Taft came from Whitelaw Reid, whose ambassadorship to Great Britain continued through the Roosevelt to the Taft administration. In his earliest letter to the first lady he explained,

> The President encouraged me to think it might help you while away the tedium of convalescence, before returning to Washington to take up the arduous duties of the next season, if I sent you an occasional letter of inside news and gossip about English politics and politicians.[60]

He also wrote to Mrs. Taft of correspondence from Sir Arthur Conan Doyle "reinforcing his book about the Congo atrocities" and of violent demonstrations he witnessed in support of woman suffrage in England.[61] Reid's letters abound in stories about well-known British personalities such as labor leader John Burns and Chancellor Lloyd George.

Reid continued to relate stories about royalty, but his hobnobbing with the British upper class was not as welcome as he might have hoped, and the president wrote to Nellie, "I see that Reid is carrying on high-jinks over in London entertaining the King and eighteen different royalties at Devonshire House, and that he is going to have the King at a weekend down at Wrest Park. This is all very fine, but it doesn't seem to me to be adding in the slightest to the usefulness of our representative in London."[62]

The president's letters to his wife deal with political maneuvering for such bills as the Payne-Aldrich Tariff, disagreements among the members of the Republican Party, grumbling over the Pinchot-Ballinger affair, and foreign relations, especially with Mexico and Canada. Her knowledge and interests apparently gave her tremendous private influence in a time not yet ready for publicly acknowledged political influence by women, particularly women married to presidents.

III

After the defeat of William Howard Taft in 1912, the "quiet dignity" that had characterized the style of Edith Roosevelt returned to the White House with Ellen Wilson's brief tenure as first lady. Bright's disease, a kidney ailment, claimed her life seventeen months after she, Woodrow Wilson, and their three daughters moved into the White House.

Ellen Louise Axson was born on May 15, 1860, in Savannah, Georgia, the daughter and granddaughter of Presbyterian ministers. She spent the greater period of her early life in Rome, Georgia, and graduated from the Female College there in 1876. Her extraordinary artistic talent was evident early on, and she would later study for a year at the Art Students' League in New York City.

Unlike the image of the Victorian lady, she was independent-minded, craved intellectual stimulation, and shunned the idea of marriage, counseling a friend, "Use all your faculties before beginning to yield to a man's fascinations."[63] One observer decided that if Ellen Axson married at all, it would probably be to "an insignificant man" because, it was reasoned, "bright people rarely ever married people who were their equal in intellect."[64]

In April 1883, however, Ellen Louise Axson met her intellectual soulmate, and by September she and Woodrow Wilson were engaged to be married. Wilson himself seemed intimidated by her intellectual prowess and chided her, "I hope you don't know much about the Constitution of the United States, for I know marvelously little about art and if you know both subjects how am I to be head of the house?"[65] Although Ellen Axson struggled with her own desire to advance her artistic skills, she finally decided that complete devotion to art was selfish and instead invested her energies in Wilson's career, which was already beginning to show promise.[66] Ellen Wilson did not completely give up her artistic endeavors, however, and while her husband was at Princeton University, she began taking lessons again and eventually exhibited her work on a number of occasions thereafter, even when she was first lady.

The papers of Woodrow Wilson in the Manuscript Division of the Library of Congress contain information about Ellen Wilson's early years as well as her life in the White House. The collection also includes papers of the Axson family dating from the mid-nineteenth century. Sermons of her father, Samuel Edward Axson, childhood letters from friends dating from 1870, and an early sketch book (ca. 1883–84) are among the items documenting the period before her marriage. There are approximately one thousand entries in the index to the Woodrow Wilson Papers that identify specific items written by or to his wife, roughly a tenth of which are letters and other material derived from her tenure in the White House. Further information about her can be found elsewhere in the collection, such as in the clippings in Series 9.

Shortly before Wilson entered the White House, Mrs. Wilson wrote to President Taft thanking him for providing her with information that would ease the move to Washington, and adding, "I am naturally the most unambitious of women and life in the White House has no attractions for me! Quite the contrary in fact!"[67]

To ease the burden of the numerous responsibilities of the first lady, Ellen Wilson brought Woodrow's cousin, Helen Woodrow Bones, to the White House to serve as private secretary. Helen Bones "took care of all her personal correspondence" and "managed the private account books."[68] Mrs. Wilson also rehired Isabelle Hagner, the efficient and well-liked secretary first employed by Edith Roosevelt, to handle social activities for herself and her daughters. Miss Hagner introduced them "to the mysteries of Washington etiquette, and solved all the problems of precedence."[69]

As with all first ladies, correspondents regularly requested Mrs. Wilson to intercede with her husband on their behalf. A number of these requests related to the perceived dominance of the so-called "Catholic Hierarchy" in his administration—a charge pointed at Joseph Tumulty, the president's private secretary. For instance, she was asked to use her influence to "prevent the appointment of Charles W. Darr," a Catholic, who was a candidate for the position of

Ellen Louise Axson (1860–1914), first wife of Woodrow Wilson, depicted here with her husband and daughters Jessie, Margaret, and Eleanor, October 1912. Mrs. Wilson ventured into Washington's slums and worked to improve housing for blacks in the city.

commissioner of the District of Columbia. The petitioner feared that if Darr should receive the appointment, "it would be useless for a Protestant to apply for a position or anything else, and be able to receive it."[70]

Similar requests were received when James M. Lynch was being considered to head the Government Printing Office. One writer, a woman, began, "I am writing this letter to you, because I fear if addressed to your husband it might never pass beyond the hands of a Catholic secretary." She went on, "The President's secretary is already feared—not in himself—he seems to be a worthy man—but on account of what he stands for in religious matters—it is that 'power behind the throne.' " In addition, the writer believed that the Government Printing Office was "considered already to be in control of the Catholics."[71] Another opponent of Lynch's appointment claimed that the candidate was a "broad man in politics, but . . . very narrow in religious matters," being "a Romanist, a worshipper of the Tyrant upon the Tiber."[72] Other reasons were given for opposition to Lynch's appointment. In one letter he was denounced as "a member of the Elks, a secret association" known to dispense drinks on the Sabbath.[73]

Although Ellen Wilson received letters concerning a number of issues from woman suffrage to the tariff, there were two areas in which she took a special interest—better working conditions for government employees and slum clearance of the alleys of the District of Columbia. Both of these matters were brought to her attention by Charlotte E. Hopkins of the Women's Welfare Department of the National Civic Federation.[74] The first lady personally visited the Post Office Department and the Government Printing Office and requested such improvements as restrooms for the women employees, individual drinking cups, better emergency hospital facilities, and a restaurant where employees could purchase food at nominal cost.[75] When she found that her request had not been acted upon, she confronted Colonel House, her husband's chief adviser, and elicited a promise from him to investigate the matter.[76]

Her major public achievement was the passage of a bill to eliminate slum dwellings in alleys in the District of Columbia and "provide sanitary homes at reasonable rental" for persons displaced.[77] She gave high visibility and prestige to that project by inviting members of the Committee of Fifty, which was charged with drafting the alley bill, to the White House and by being present at their meetings.[78] On the morning of August 6, 1914, as she lay dying, the first lady told the president that she could "go away more cheerfully" knowing that the alley bill had passed.[79] Almost simultaneously, Joseph Tumulty was taking this plea to the Capitol, where Congress made her wish a reality in time for the first lady to be informed that the bill had passed.[80]

Years later, Eleanor Wilson McAdoo described her mother as "a quiet, gentle, unassuming woman who avoided the limelight so successfully that she has been almost forgotten." Yet it was Ellen Wilson's "selfless love, wise advice and constant encouragement" that contributed greatly to her husband's successful career.[81]

IV

In March 1915, almost eight months after Ellen Wilson's death, Woodrow Wilson met and fell in love with a prosperous widow. Edith Bolling Galt ran the successful jewelry store she had inherited from her husband. Since his death, she had been managing the business and traveling abroad extensively. Initially resisting Wilson's open and passionate pleas for marriage, she finally succumbed and devoted the rest of her life to him and his ideals.

Born in 1872 in Wytheville, Virginia, Edith Bolling was the seventh of eleven children born to William Holcombe and Sallie White Bolling, only nine of whom survived to adulthood. The family lived in what has been called "genteel poverty," as their land holdings and other property had been devastated by the Civil War.[82] Edith Bolling contended that she could trace her ancestry back to Pocahontas, and the public awareness of this ancestry prompted an outpouring of mail to her on various aspects of Indian life. Educated primarily at home by her paternal grandmother and her father, who was a lawyer and circuit court judge, she later attended one year each at Martha Washington College in Abingdon, Virginia, and at the Powell School in Richmond. In 1890 she met Norman Galt, a cousin of her brother-in-law, and they were married six years later. Edith Bolling Galt had one child who died in infancy in 1903, and five years later her husband died. She was a close friend of the fiancee of Cary T. Grayson, Woodrow Wilson's personal physician, and it was through him that she met the president.

The intensity of their romance can be seen in the daily letters written from April to December of 1915, when marriage vows were exchanged at the bride's home in Washington. Candid in his feelings, Wilson had proclaimed early in their relationship, "There is no one else in the world for me now—there is nothing worthwhile but love. Nothing else gives life, or confidence, or joy in action. A man is not sufficient by himself, whatever his strength and courage. He is maimed and incomplete without his mate, his heart's companion, the dear one to whom he is lover and comrade."[83] Edith's replies were equally moving: "Oh, how I longed to put both my arms 'round your neck and beg you to let me take part of the weariness, part of the responsibility and try to make you forget everything else in the assurance of the love and loyalty that fills my heart."[84]

It is unlikely that Edith Bolling Galt realized initially how much of the "responsibility" and "weariness" she would be shouldering. Evidence of the burden she had to bear can be seen in the Woodrow Wilson Papers. Her correspondence consists of more than ten thousand letters and other materials dated before, during, and after her years in the White House. Of particular interest are the scrapbooks in Series 9, which provide a history of the Wilson White House years. The postpresidential period is marked by correspondence dating to 1955 relating to her husband and to the publication of her memoir. In addition, there is a separate collection of Edith Bolling Wilson's own papers numbering approximately nineteen thousand items dating from 1893 to 1961, the year of her death. Aside from family correspondence, the bulk of the collection dates from the president's death in 1924 and includes correspondence with many of their close friends, political allies, and world leaders.

From the beginning of their romance, Wilson began to share his entire world with Mrs. Galt, not only writing of his love for her but also discussing the state of world affairs. Shortly after their first meeting, the *Lusitania* was sunk by the Germans. Wilson and the secretary of state, William Jennings Bryan, disagreed on foreign policy, and he wrote to Galt, "It was your friend W.J.B. who took the ground that we must let Americans understand that they took passage on British ships, or any ships owned by belligerents, at their own risk and peril. Beware of heresies!"[85] Wilson not only wrote to his fiancee about foreign affairs, but also sent her copies of official documents and installed a private telephone line from the White House to her Dupont Circle home in northwest Washington. Eventually Edith Wilson would become a more trusted confidante than Colonel Edward House or Joseph Tumulty.

Prior to her marriage, Galt began receiving mail as if she were the first lady. When her engagement to Wilson was announced in October, office seekers, individuals requesting pardons and interviews, and those offering political advice sought her intercession to bring their interests to the president. One man wrote that he was sending his correspondence to Galt because she was "as much interested in Mr. Wilson, as Mr. Wilson was in himself."[86] Another came from a woman seeking the position of social secretary to the future first lady.

Isabelle Hagner, who had stayed on at the White House after the death of Ellen Wilson, had announced her plans to marry. Hagner convinced her friend Edith Benham (later Helm), who had wide experience as a social secretary, to replace her. Benham later recalled that she had not wanted the job initially, for she could make more money working only in the winter at less demanding positions and still have the summers free.[87] Not only did Benham handle social functions at the White House, she accompanied the president and Mrs. Wilson to Paris for the peace conference in 1919, taking copious notes that were later published. The strain of the last years in the White House eventually caused a nervous collapse, and Benham left on March 4, 1920, under doctors' orders.[88] Mrs. Wilson took over the work with the assistance of Frank Magee, who had served as a typist for the social secretary.[89]

The first lady's good rapport with some of the president's cabinet members is documented in the collection. Franklin K. Lane, secretary of the interior, sent Edith Wilson a copy of a letter to him with the covering statement, "Here is a letter that places a terrible power in my hands. If at any time you wish this power exercised I shall not hesitate to do my duty. Yours for the enforcement of the law."[90] The letter was from a woman claiming to be a descendant of Pocahontas, as was the first lady, and stated that the president had broken the law by serving "wine and liquors to Mrs. Wilson" since it was illegal to give, sell, or in any way distribute such beverages to Indians. The writer demanded that the president be arrested immediately "according to the laws of these United States of America."[91] The first lady responded:

> My dear Mr. Sec=
>
> I have just read Mrs.——letter to the accused & he insists that he thinks the law she speaks of applies only to those of my tribe living on a Reservation & is not applicable to *us* when we are at large—However, I feel sure you will agree with me that he is only trying to evade the Laws of these United States framed to protect the poor Indian—However owing to the fact that the accused is now rendering patriotic service—would suggest that he be warned against further offense—and that we hold this weapen [*sic*] given into our hands for future use should he become irresponsible.[92]

Most of the letters to Mrs. Wilson concerning Indian affairs were either more serious or more pleasant in nature. One concerned congressional appropriations for the Seminoles; another was enclosed with a handbag made by a member of the Menominee tribe.[93]

The entry of the United States into World War I on April 6, 1917, brought a dramatic change to the White House. The first lady immersed herself in war work, sewing pajamas, sheets, and pillow cases and knitting trench helmets to be distributed by the Red Cross. She also worked at the Red Cross canteen near Union Station, distributing coffee and sandwiches to the soldiers as they disembarked briefly from the trains carrying them to training camps. But most important, she spent hours helping the president with his communiques, working far into the night coding and decoding messages.

In public she was seen constantly by his side. As one newspaper columnist wrote, "She is just an American woman—of the type our mothers were. The masculine dash and manners of many of our modern women are entirely lacking in this lady of the White House. She is primarily a helpmeet and a homemaker. . . Surely she is closer to her husband in this great struggle than the First Lady of Germany is to the Prussian War Lord."[94]

Following the armistice that ended the hostilities in Europe, the first lady and her social secretary accompanied the president on both of his trips to Europe for the Paris Peace Conference. At home, the president of the League of American Pen Women wrote to Miss Benham, "I feel I am expressing the sentiments of the organization I represent in saying how proud and happy we are to have the women of America represented by Mrs. Wilson, who will do us more credit than any one else possibly could."[95] During this time, the first lady received letters from members of the royal families of Europe as well as political leaders. On returning home, she also accompanied Wilson on his trip to the West to win the support of the American people for the treaty and the establishment of the League of Nations, for which he had so passionately worked. In the American press the first lady was applauded for her constant presence at her husband's side and her refusal of invitations to functions that would pay her any special honor.[96]

A little over three weeks into the trip, on September 25, 1919, the president collapsed and was rushed back to Washington. A week later he suffered a stroke which left him paralyzed on the left side. The first lady would begin what she later called her "stewardship" of the White House for the remaining seventeen months of the Wilson administration.

The extent of this stewardship has been the subject of great interest to historians. In her memoir, Edith Wilson asserted,

> I, myself, never made a single decision regarding the disposition of public affairs. The only decision that was mine was what was important and what was not, and the very important decision of when to present matters to my husband.[97]

And indeed, there is evidence of that assertion in the Wilson Papers and also in the Tumulty Papers housed in the Manuscript Division.

There are numerous memorandums from the president's secretary, Joseph Tumulty, to the first lady requesting that she seek an opinion or statement from the president on various matters. Very little business occurred in October and November of 1919, and Tumulty sent a memorandum to Mrs. Wilson on December 18 listing the areas where action was needed, including a statement relating to the seizure of the railroads by the government; the selection of a commission to settle a coal miners' strike; the appointment to the cabinet of secretaries for the departments of the Treasury and Interior; and also appointments to the Civil Service Commission, Federal Trade Commission, Interstate Commerce Commission, U.S. Shipping Board, and U.S. Tariff Commission, as well as to many other positions and diplomatic posts.[98] On December 24, in a very shaky hand, Woodrow Wilson responded, "*must* let me alone about the RRs. I've announced that the roads go back to their owners Jany lst. and that cannot be altered."[99] Many of the responses, however, were in Edith Wilson's handwriting and generally began, "The President says," followed by a brief response agreeing, disagreeing, asking for additional information, or requesting that the appropriate papers be forwarded to finalize an action.

The first lady also served as the president's representative in discussions with department heads and other officials. When Franklin K. Lane resigned as secretary of the interior, Mrs. Wilson called John Barton Payne to the White House and, over tea, offered him the position. "The President has asked Judge

Edith Bolling Galt Wilson (1872–1961), Wilson's second wife, and her husband at the 1915 World Series. After the president suffered a disabling stroke, she remained his constant attendant and took over many routine duties of government.

Payne of the Shipping Board to become Sec. of the Interior & he has accepted," she wrote to Tumulty. "Will you send him over the nomination to sign–?"[100]

There was no question that her role was controversial. One senator claimed that the United States had a "Petticoat government" while others called her the "Presidentress," "Lady President," "First Woman President," "Iron Queen," and other epithets.[101] By February of 1920 newspapers were calling her the "Acting Ruler" and stating that she had been "acting President of the United States since October."[102] One article indicated that she was a "buffer—and a very effective one—between her invalid husband and the great affairs of State." The article was complimentary to Mrs. Wilson, stating that "Although the tongues of Washington gossip were wagging vigorously, no suggestion is heard that Mrs. Wilson is not proving a capable 'President.' "[103] In March an article in *Collier's* noted that although Mrs. Wilson was "never an ardent suffragist herself," she had "proved herself the finest argument for suffrage that any woman by her work" had exhibited. It noted her experience as a businesswoman and found it acceptable that she "took the woman's way" by conducting business over tea and cakes. Even her appearance, which had always received the highest praise in the press, was a subject for discussion. As one journalist put it, "Her morning outfit of crisp blouse and walking skirt, or white linen frock, indicates her knowledge of dress appropriate to her job."[104]

There were those who felt that the first lady deserved great admiration for her role even though they found the idea of "a President Jane Adams [*sic*] or a President Carrie Chapman Catt" to be "annoying" and "ridiculous."[105] By September, Senator Carter Glass was quoted as saying, "I confess I was amazed at the promptness with which Mrs. Wilson renounced every other interest in life and from the moment of the President's illness applied herself to helping and sustaining him. She showed from the first a grasp of affairs that surprised us all."[106]

Items among the Wilson Papers for the period from the president's initial illness until the end of his second term document the expanding role of the first lady in public affairs. However, there are also glimpses of the Wilsons' personal life as she worked hard to build the president's strength both physically and emotionally. "I can not express the love & gratification this thrills me with," she wrote in May 1920, "but I believe you know—and, because you know, you will struggle on and on until the Valley of Sorrow is over and together we will stand on the hieght [*sic*] and look back upon it—Both stronger for the lesson it has taught—and surer of our great love—[107]

Continuing to attempt to bolster his morale against the numerous disappointments and defeats he suffered at this time, she wrote again two weeks later:

> June 5 - 1920
>
> My Own Precious One =
> When you asked me if I had faith in you it was like asking if I believed the Sun gave light—You are to me the tangible evidence of all that is strong—fine and true! I trust you unquestionly and have faith in you beyond words to express.
>
> Sometimes you tell me I am Strong or, as you put it, "great"—don't you see little Boy—that it is the contact with you and your greatness that lifts me up and if there is merit in me—it is because I am your mirror in which your finess is reflected.
>
> You are so splendid your self that the very fact makes you blind to itself and I would not have it otherwise.
>
> Always remember dear One that you are not very Strong your self but that by your example you make us So—and that any one who is with you as I have been absorbs all wholesome things and become better from the inspiration!
>
> I love you—always
> E.B.W.[108]

On March 4, 1921, Edith Wilson retired from public life with her husband. She spent the rest of her life promoting his work and ideals. When her memoir was published, first in serial installments in the *Saturday Evening Post* and later as a book, there were mixed reactions. Many praised it as a biography of her husband. Some criticized it for being too personal. Others felt it was inaccurate. Irita Van Doren, in her radio broadcast of March 24, 1939, noted that reaction to the publication ran "the whole gamut of approval and disapproval" and indicated that this was "proof of only one thing—the vitality and fascination of the record, whatever conclusions you draw from it."[109]

V

This fascination with the record is frustrated somewhat by the fragmentary documentation of the lives of these early twentieth-century first ladies. The fact that they did not routinely save copies of their outgoing letters presents a special challenge to researchers, who must search the papers of many other individuals to locate material relevant to this topic. In the Manuscript Division there are many letters from Edith Kermit Roosevelt among the papers of Kermit and Theodore Roosevelt, Jr. More about Helen Herron Taft may be found among the papers of her children, Robert and Charles Taft and Helen Taft Manning. In addition, there are records kept by those who worked closely with the presidential families such as Irwin (Ike) Hoover, head usher at the White House during these administrations, and Edith Benham Helm, social secretary for Edith Bolling Wilson and later for Eleanor Roosevelt. References to these collections and to the papers of many public officials and personal friends can be found in a special index to the letters and other documents of first ladies available in the Manuscript Division. Thus researchers may study a more complete record to draw their conclusions about the role and place of the first ladies in American history. It is obvious that these four first ladies would have claimed that they sought no public role, and would have denied their political influence; however, the records suggest otherwise. Documentation of their interests, activities, and involvement in their husbands' lives indicates a greater role in the nation's history than would otherwise be evident had these records not been preserved for research.

Notes

[1]Edith Kermit Roosevelt and Kermit Roosevelt, *American Backlogs: The Story of Gertrude Tyler and Her Family, 1660–1860* (1928), presents a detailed account of Edith Roosevelt's maternal side of the family.

[2]Theodore Roosevelt diary entry, Feb. 14, 1884, Series 8, Theodore Roosevelt Papers, Manuscript Division, Library of Congress, Washington, DC.

[3]Betty Boyd Caroli, *First Ladies* (1987), p. 117. See also Sylvia Jukes Morris, *Edith Kermit Roosevelt: Portrait of a First Lady* (1980), p. 221.

[4]Morris, *Edith Kermit Roosevelt*, p. 457.

[5]Ibid., p. 457–458.

[6]Josephine Shaw Lowell to Edith Kermit Carow Roosevelt, Feb. 13, 1902, Series 1, vol. 61, TR Papers, Ms. Div., LC. See also *Index to the Papers of Theodore Roosevelt* (1969), p. xii, for a discussion of the removal of routine or unimportant documents.

[7]Volumes 105–107, Series 2, TR Papers, Ms. Div., LC.

[8]Morris, *Edith Kermit Roosevelt*, p. 226.

[9]Mary Randolph, *Presidents and First Ladies* (1936), p. 182.

[10]Lawrence F. Abbott, ed., *The Letters of Archie Butt, Personal Aid to President Roosevelt* (1924), p. 53.

[11]Randolph, *Presidents and First Ladies*, p. 183–184.

[12]Helena McCarthy, "Why Mrs. Roosevelt Has Not Broken Down," *Ladies Home Journal* (Oct. 1908), p. 25.

[13]Ibid.

[14]Morris, *Edith Kermit Roosevelt*, p. 260.

[15]EKCR to Miss Bangs, Sept. 6, 1902, Series 2, vol. 106, TR Papers, Ms. Div., LC.

[16]EKCR to Kermit Roosevelt, Nov. 1, 1905, container 10, Kermit Roosevelt Papers, Ms. Div., LC.

[17]EKCR to Miss Fitzgerald, Feb. 26, 1905, Series 2, vol. 107, TR Papers, Ms. Div., LC.

[18]Warren S. Young to B. F. Barnes, Apr. 22, 1907, Series 2, vol. 107, TR Papers, Ms. Div., LC.

[19]Bingham Duncan, *Whitelaw Reid: Journalist, Politician, Diplomat* (1975), p. 220.

[20]Ibid.

[21]EKCR to Elisabeth Mills Reid, Mar. 31, 1921, container B12, Reid Family Papers, Ms. Div., LC.

[22]Whitelaw Reid to EKCR, Apr. 12, 1906, Series 1, TR Papers, Ms. Div., LC.

[23]Whitelaw Reid to EKCR, June 1, 1906, Series 1, TR Papers, Ms. Div., LC.

[24]Morris, *Edith Kermit Roosevelt*, p. 233.

[25]Cecil Spring-Rice to EKCR, Dec. 9, 1903, Series 1, TR Papers, Ms. Div., LC.

[26]Cecil Spring-Rice to EKCR, Mar. 29, 1905, Series 1, TR Papers, Ms. Div., LC.

[27]Owen Wister to TR, Sept. 16, 1903, Series 1, TR Papers, Ms. Div., LC.

[28]Morris, *Edith Kermit Roosevelt*, p. 268.

[29]*The Troy Daily Times*, Feb. 8, 1902, Personal Scrapbook no. 1, p. 143, Series 15, TR Papers, Ms. Div., LC.

[30]Jacob A. Riis, "Mrs. Roosevelt and Her Children," *Ladies Home Journal* (Aug. 1902), p. 5, and Morris, *Edith Kermit Roosevelt*, p. 3.

[31]Morris, p. 502.

[32]Ishbel Ross, *An American Family: The Tafts, 1678 to 1964* (1964), p. 150.

[33]Mrs. William Howard Taft, *Recollections of Full Years* (1914), pp. 331–332.

[34]Ibid., p. 5.

[35]Stanley I. Kutler, biographical essay in *Notable American Women* (1971), p. 420.

[36]Taft, *Recollections*, p. 5.

[37]Ibid., p. 6.

[38]Ibid., p. 7–8.

[39]Ross, *An American Family*, p. 95.

[40]Ibid., p. 97.

[41]Taft, *Recollections*, p. 365.

[42]William Howard Taft to Helen Herron Taft, Mar. 25, 1909, Presidential Letter book, vol. 2, p. 116, Series 8, William Howard Taft Papers, Ms. Div., LC.

[43]Ross, *An American Family*, p. 214.

[44]Ibid., p. 236.

[45]Ibid., p. 215–216.

[46]Helen Herron Taft diary, Sept. 5, 1879, Diary 1879–80, Series 11, WHT Papers, Ms. Div., LC.

[47]Ross, *An American Family*, p. 239.

[48]Mary Dandridge Spiers to William Howard Taft, Apr. 15, 1910, Series 5, case file 3567, WHT Papers, Ms. Div., LC.

[49]HHT to WHT [1909], Series 3, WHT Papers, Ms. Div., LC.

[50]Ross, *An American Family*, p. 237.

[51]Frank H. McManigal to HHT [Mar. 21, 1909], Series 5, case file 2199, WHT Papers, Ms. Div., LC.

[52]There are many examples of letters that address the issue of public image of Helen Taft as first lady in Series 5, case files 752, 1777, 2253, 3526, 4143, 4346, and others, WHT Papers, Ms. Div., LC.

[53]Alice M. Ball to HHT, July 4, 1909, Series 5, case file 109, WHT Papers, Ms. Div., LC.

[54]Note to WHT, ca. July 4, 1909, mounting #8144, Series 5, case file 109, WHT Papers, Ms. Div., LC.

[55]Mrs. Pincus Schein to HHT, Mar. 9, 1910, and Charles Nagel to WHT, Mar. 15, 1910, Series 5, case file 3316, WHT Papers, Ms. Div., LC.

[56]Mrs. Anna E. Murray to HHT, Mar. 6, 1910, Series 5, case file 2553, WHT Papers, Ms. Div., LC.

[57]"President Heeds Mrs. Taft's Plea for Mercy for Condemned Man," clipping, ca. Aug. 1909, mounting #3186, Series 5, case file 3329, WHT Papers, Ms. Div., LC.

[58]Frances H. Ensign et al. to HHT, Apr. 2, 1909, Series 5, case file 2999, WHT Papers, Ms. Div., LC. See also Series 5, case files 3351 and 4133, ibid.

[59]Note from HHT to Alice Blech on letter of M. D. Stout to HHT, Apr. 7 [1909?], Series 5, case file 2999, WHT Papers, Ms. Div., LC.

[60]Whitelaw Reid to HHT, Oct. 12, 1909, Series 3, WHT Papers, Ms. Div., LC.

[61]Ibid.

[62]WHT to HHT, July 11, 1909, Series 8, Presidential Letter books, vol. 5, p. 177, WHT Papers, Ms. Div., LC.

[63]Frances Wright Saunders, *First Lady Between Two Worlds: Ellen Axson Wilson* (1985), p. 28.

[64]Elizabeth Leith Adams to Ellen Louise Axson, Christmas, 1880, Series 2, Woodrow Wilson Papers, Ms. Div., LC.

[65]Arthur S. Link, ed., *The Papers of Woodrow Wilson* (1967), vol. 3, p. 133.

[66]Saunders, *First Lady Between Two Worlds*, p. 58.

[67]Ellen Louise Axson Wilson to WHT, Jan. 10, 1913, Series 7, case file 723, WHT Papers, Ms. Div., LC.

[68]Eleanor Wilson McAdoo, *The Woodrow Wilsons* (1937), p. 238.

[69]Ibid., p. 228.

[70]Anonymous to ELAW, Mar. 12, 1913, Series 4, case file 84A16, WW Papers, Ms. Div., LC.

[71]Mary A. Ledburn to ELAW, Apr. 14, 1913, Series 4, case file 4A25, WW Papers, Ms. Div., LC.

[72]J. D. Lyon to ELAW, Apr. 15, 1913, Series 4, case file 4A25, WW Papers, Ms. Div., LC.

[73]"A Temperate Printer" to ELAW, Apr. 17, 1913, Series 4, case file 4A25, WW Papers, Ms. Div., LC.

[74]Charlotte E. Hopkins to ELAW, Mar. 31, 1913, Series 2, WW Papers, Ms. Div., LC.

[75][C. Ford] to ELAW, Jan. 29, 1914, Series 4, WW Papers, Ms. Div., LC.

[76]Saunders, *First Lady Between Two Worlds*, p. 246.

[77]Edith E. Wood to ELAW, Sept. 25, 1913, Series 4, case file 84, WW Papers, Ms. Div., LC.

[78]Saunders, p. 245–246.

[79]Ibid., p. 276.

[80]Ibid.

[81]Eleanor Wilson McAdoo, ed., *The Priceless Gift: The Love Letters of Woodrow Wilson and Ellen Axson Wilson* (1962), p. ix.

[82]Arthur S. Link, biographical essay on Edith Bolling Galt Wilson in *Notable American Women: The Modern Period* (1980), p. 739.

[83]WW to Edith Bolling Galt, June 1, 1915, Series 20, WW Papers, Ms. Div., LC.

[84]EBG to WW, June 10, 1915, ibid.

[85]WW to EBG, Aug. 22, 1915, ibid.

[86]Albertus E. Hanson to EBG, Dec. 5, 1915, Series 2, WW Papers, Ms. Div., LC.

[87]Edith Benham Helm, *The Captains and the Kings* (1954), p. 46. See also "Social Secretary Has No Sinecure," *The Evening Star*, Series 9, vol. 2, p. 11, WW Papers, Ms. Div., LC.

[88]Edith Bolling Wilson, My *Memoir* (1938), p. 320, and Helm, *The Captains and the Kings*, p. 125.

[89]Wilson, My *Memoir*, p. 230.

[90]Franklin K. Lane to Edith Bolling Galt Wilson, n.d., Series 9, vol. 2, p. 21, WW Papers, Ms. Div., LC.

[91]May H. Gonzalez to Secretary of Interior, Apr. 10, 1917, Series 9, vol. 2, p. 21, WW Papers, Ms. Div., LC.

[92]EBGW to Franklin K. Lane, n.d., ibid.

[93]Duncan Fletcher to Edith Benham, Feb. 11, 1916, Series 9, vol. 1, p. 136 and Sarah Wilber to EBGW, Apr. 27, 1917, Series 9, vol. 2, p. 23, WW Papers, Ms. Div., LC.

[94]"Mrs. Wilson Helpmeet and Homemaker for President; Is Aiding Him in War Duties," clipping [ca. July 1917], Series 9, vol. 2, p. 38, WW Papers, Ms. Div., LC.

[95]Margaret E. Pearson to Edith Benham, Jan. 20, 1919, Series 9, vol. 3, p. 61, WW Papers, Ms. Div., LC.

[96]"Introducing the First Lady of the Land, in City Today," *The Spokane Press*, Sept. 12, 1919, Series 9, vol. 4, p. 218, WW Papers, Ms. Div., LC.

[97]Wilson, My *Memoir*, p. 289.

[98]Joseph P. Tumulty to EBGW, Dec. 18, 1919, Edith Wilson file, Special Correspondence series, container 46, Joseph P. Tumulty Papers, Ms. Div., LC.

[99]WW to Joseph P. Tumulty, Dec. 24, 1919, Woodrow Wilson file, Special Correspondence series, Joseph P. Tumulty

Papers, Ms. Div., LC.

[100]EBGW to Joseph P. Tumulty, Feb. 20, 1920, Series 4, case file 69, WW Papers, Ms. Div., LC.

[101]Ishbel Ross, *Power With Grace: The Life Story of Mrs. Woodrow Wilson* (1975), p. 201.

[102]"Mrs. Wilson as Acting Ruler," *Daily Mail* (London), Feb. 22, 1920, Series 9, vol. 5, p. 3, WW Papers, Ms. Div., LC.

[103]Ibid.

[104]Robert J. Bender, "Signed—Edith Bolling Wilson," *Collier's* (Mar. 6, 1920), p. 6. (Also in Series 9, vol. 5, p. 6, WW Papers, Ms. Div., LC.)

[105]"The First Lady," Mar. 16, 1920, *Star* (Baltimore), Series 9, vol. 5, p. 7, WW Papers, Ms. Div., LC.

[106]"Mrs. Wilson Finds Real Happiness Nursing President Back to Health," Sept. 4, 1920, Series 9, Vol. 5, p. 20, WW Papers, Ms. Div., LC.

[107]EBGW to WW, May 24, 1920, Series 20, WW Papers, Ms. Div., LC.

[108]EBGW to WW, June 5, 1920, ibid.

[109]Transcript of NBC radio broadcast of Irita Van Doren, Mar. 24, 1939, enclosed in letter from D. L. Saunders to Marquis James, Mar. 27, 1939, Memoirs of Eidth Bolling Wilson file, container 25, Marquis James Papers, Ms. Div., LC.

Not One to Stay at Home

The Papers of Lou Henry Hoover

By Dale C. Mayer

Dedicated to service and philanthropy, Lou Henry Hoover was respectfully described by her husband as "a symbol of everything wholesome in American life."

Considering our superficial acquaintance with earlier first ladies, it is not surprising that Lou Henry Hoover continues to be one of the more obscure and little-known first ladies. Our fascination with Martha Washington, Dolley Madison, and Mary Todd Lincoln is frustrated by their failure to have preserved many of their personal papers, an unfortunate situation that is mirrored in the dispersal and relative scarcity of presidential papers prior to those of William Howard Taft.

More extensive documentation of first ladies' activities begins with Edith Galt Wilson, whose papers amount to less than 20,000 items occupying 27 linear feet of shelving. The Lou Henry Hoover papers (141 linear feet and over 220,000 items) constitute the earliest large-scale collection documenting the day-to-day activities of a first lady.

Unlike the papers of her predecessors, Mrs. Hoover's papers provide coverage of her entire life from her teenage years in the 1890s through her death in 1944. Opened to scholars and the public alike in the spring of 1985, the papers offer many opportunities to assess her place in women's history and provide innumerable insights into the personality and fascinating life of one of the more intriguing women ever to have presided as first lady.

Because the papers have been only recently opened for research, it is not possible to anticipate the judgment of the historical community. It is possible, however, to discuss some of the interesting things that have already been discovered about Mrs. Hoover and her three major interests in life: education, service to others, and the outdoors.

While these interests surface in many of her letters to friends and associates, one letter, written in November 1914 before rejoining her husband in London, mentions all three. World War I had begun four months earlier, and Mrs. Hoover was well aware of the dangers of a trip through submarine-infested waters. Before sailing, she wrote a long letter to Jackson Reynolds, a Stanford classmate, asking him to oversee the education of her sons in case anything should happen to her or her husband during their wartime travels.

> I do not ask you to take them into your home . . . But do direct their education and let them . . . get your ideals of the world. . . . I think a few years as little boys in California—where they have plenty of outdoors and

> village life—might be very good . . . The ambition to do, to accomplish, irrespective of its measure in money or fame, is what should be inculcated . . . I know you have the right balance to make good men out of my boys, physically, intellectually, and in the yet higher things. But I hope you will never get a chance to get a try at it.[1]

In expressing her concerns and hopes for her sons, Mrs. Hoover indicated the value she placed on a good education, outdoor recreation, and a life of service to others.

Mrs. Hoover's interest in education was demonstrated on many occasions. Some of her earliest letters and essays, which date from the 1890s, clearly indicate her determination to prepare herself for a full and useful life. For a time she considered becoming a teacher and attended the Normal School in San Jose, California. In 1892, however, she attended a lecture on geology given by John Caspar Branner, a visiting professor from Stanford University, that changed her life.

Having spent much of her time on hiking trips observing rock strata and formations, she found Professor Branner's talk fascinating. When Branner assured her that geologists spend a great deal of time working outdoors, the combination was too good to resist. The following fall she transferred to Stanford where the persuasive Branner soon introduced her to his lab assistant, a shy senior named Herbert Hoover.

In 1898 Lou Henry graduated from Stanford University. So far as can be determined, she was the first woman in the United States to get a degree in geology. This unusual career choice, plus some recently discovered correspondence and essays from that period, provides early evidence of her deeply ingrained individuality and encourages speculation about her stand on career choices for women.

Writing to a friend after graduation from Stanford, she wondered what life would hold for her and expressed her impatience to get on with her life and career. Referring to her parents, who had so often supported and encouraged her, she had to admit that "they would not want me to stay meekly at home."[2]

By the time she left Stanford, many of her views on the purpose and function of education and its role in shaping a productive life were firmly established. Much of this was due to the influence of Branner and his colleagues at Stanford, and the rest was due to the earlier influence of her Quaker relatives and friends. As indicated in her 1914 letter to Jackson Reynolds, she believed that education should do more than just equip a person to make a comfortable living. Ideally, teachers should have a positive influence on their students, motivating them to use their talents and abilities in the service of others. This concept of service remained a key ingredient in her personal philosophy and shaped many of her subsequent actions.

Her reading and experiences also led Mrs. Hoover to the conviction that education was essential to America's continued progress and evolution as a free society. She believed that American society would continue to improve only if each individual contributed his or her share, and that those contributions could be enhanced and enlarged by education.

Although Mrs. Hoover often wrote and spoke about the importance of education and public service, one letter in particular, written in 1922 to Sen.

With mortar and pestle, Lou Henry works in the chemistry lab at Stanford, where she caught the attention of a shy student named Herbert Hoover. In 1898 she became the first woman in the United States to receive a degree in geology.

Frank B. Kellogg, reveals an important part of her educational philosophy. Senator Kellogg was on the Senate oversight committee for the operation of the District of Columbia, which was responsible for the management of public schools in the District. While protesting the crowded conditions that had necessitated split shifts at her son's high school, Mrs. Hoover emphasized the importance of quality public education.

> There are good private schools in our country. I can afford to send my boy to them and naturally have considered them carefully. But we don't want to send him away, and he does not want to go. . . .
>
> But suppose that the conditions became such that I felt *forced* to send my boy to a private school, not alone for his sake, but in order that we might also thus make more room for the children of people who can not possibly send theirs away. This is a process already well under way. . . .

> The democracy of our school system will be destroyed, the public High Schools . . . will come to be considered for the education *only* of the children of those who *cannot* afford anything better. And we will be striking the cleavage of a money aristocracy straight down through our nation to the foundations of our educational system.[3]

One cannot help but be struck by her perception and the extent to which she grasped the significance of education in a free society.

Mrs. Hoover's contributions to the promotion of education were not confined to advice, however. During their lifetimes the Hoovers gave generously to Stanford University and frequently lent the use of their names for fund-raising drives sponsored by their alma mater. Their magnificent home was presented to the university in 1945 as a residence for the university president. In addition to their large gifts to Stanford, they also helped many students to get through college and vocational training programs.

This impromptu scholarship program began soon after their marriage. In an 1899 letter to her mother, written about six months after her marriage, Lou mentions her reluctance to spend a great deal of money on her dresses. "While I want them very nice," she wrote, "I don't want them very extravagant. For we are having plenty of expenses of our own now—not to mention our four whole people in college and two for whom we are half responsible."[4] The total amount of their giving for educational purposes will never be known because, true to the Quaker ideals that emphasize doing one's good deeds privately, they succeeded in concealing much of their generosity.

Historians and researchers who work with Mrs. Hoover's papers have already noticed her lack of pretense, her intelligence, and her kind and generous spirit. In stark contrast to the laconic, businesslike official correspondence in her husband's papers, her lively letters are like a breath of fresh air. Her sense of humor, zest for living, and concern for others are sprinkled generously through her correspondence. One phrase that occurs fairly regularly is key to understanding her. "Tell me about your good deeds," she would write to her friends. If they had nothing to report, she was not above making recommendations, which after 1917 usually involved work in the Girl Scout movement. The Girl Scouts quickly became her primary concern, and today she is best known for her contributions to that movement. It was, however, only one area in which she demonstrated her penchant for "good deeds."

When World War I broke out, tens of thousands of Americans were stranded in Europe. In the ensuing chaos, luggage was lost, tickets on German steamship lines became worthless, and London hotels briefly refused to accept even American currency. To make matters still worse, conditions in Europe's panic-stricken financial market preceding the outbreak of hostilities had provoked a British bank holiday over the weekend of August 1–3, 1914.

On Monday afternoon, August 3, Herbert Hoover received a call for assistance from his friend Robert P. Skinner, the American consul general, whose offices were besieged by nearly a thousand stranded Americans. A few hundred British pounds, which Hoover had withdrawn from his bank on Friday afternoon to pay the salaries of his office staff, were still in the office safe. Some of Hoover's American friends had taken similar precautions, and with these slender resources a committee was established to begin making loans and arranging passage so

Lou Henry Hoover and her sons Herbert and Allan pose with their jinrikisha driver in Burma. The adventurous life of a young mining engineer carried the Hoovers to such distant shores as Ceylon, Australia, Egypt, Japan, India, Siberia, and Europe.

the Americans could return home. Many of them faced a long wait, for it was the height of the tourist season and most accommodations had already been booked. In the meantime, they needed advice, reassurance, lodging, food, and clothing. These tasks were beyond the capacity of Mr. Hoover's committee, so Mrs. Hoover organized a group of American women to deal with these more immediate problems.

Eventually her committee's activities went well beyond aiding stranded Americans. As the war progressed, the committee, known as the American Women's War Relief Fund, ran field dressing stations in Belgium, operated convalescent hospitals in Britain and France, and reopened several small woolen mills in the London slums to relieve unemployment. More than 120,000 people were served by the committees the Hoovers organized, and over $1,500,000 were spent on loans and assistance of one kind or another.[5]

A few other examples demonstrate the range of Mrs. Hoover's generosity, commitment, and creativity in public service ventures. When Mr. Hoover became U.S. Food Administrator in 1917, the couple moved back to the United States. Mrs. Hoover soon discovered that many of the young women who had come to Washington to work in government offices were having a difficult time finding reasonable housing and low-cost meals. Sympathizing with them, she helped organize a club modeled on the eating and social clubs found on many college campuses. She supplied not only the organizing skills, but the start-up money as well. She rented a large house, furnished it, installed a commercial-grade kitchen, and provided housing for some fifteen to twenty young women. In the 1920s Mrs. Hoover launched a similar experiment at Stanford University when she found out that faculty members were having difficulty finding housing close to campus. Suitable housing simply was not available, so she built seven modest but comfortable homes and rented them at bargain rates that barely covered her expenses.

During the presidential years, the Hoovers also privately built a retreat in the mountains of West Virginia to escape from the heat of Washington summers. Soon after they began using the camp, they became aware that the children who lived nearby had no school. Their families were desperately poor and lived in such a remote hollow that no public school had ever been provided. Touched by the privation of these families, the Hoovers, entirely at their own expense, built a school, furnished it with modern equipment, and hired a teacher who was familiar with the special needs of Appalachian children. Mrs. Hoover also made efforts to find jobs for the children's fathers and sent gifts of food and clothing at Christmas time.

The third of Mrs. Hoover's major interests arose out of her fun-loving personality. Her pursuit of a "good time" was not entirely frivolous, however. In our day we have finally come to take very seriously her belief that outdoor recreation and activity are essential for good health. In her letters she often advised friends that outdoor activity would do wonders for their mental outlook and would allow them to resume their work with renewed vigor and productivity. She also saw to it that her sons got away from classrooms and cities to stay at their uncle's ranch, to visit their grandfather's mountain cabin, or to enjoy some fishing with their father.

Mrs. Hoover was an avid camper and hiker and continued to go camping in rugged parts of the Sierra Nevada when she was in her mid-sixties. She had learned to love the outdoors while on hiking and fishing trips with her father, and memories of those pleasant experiences provided her with powerful incentives to become involved in the development of the Girl Scout movement. She later reflected that "I was a Scout years ago, before the movement ever started, when my father took me hunting, fishing and hiking in the mountains. Then I was sorry that more girls could not have what I had. When I learned of the movement I thought, here is what I have always wanted other girls to have."[6]

Her enjoyment of the outdoors led naturally to a certain wanderlust, a love for travel that apparently was never satisfied. Beginning with their honeymoon on an ocean steamer bound for Herbert Hoover's new job in China, the couple traveled around the world several times during his career as a mining engineer and consultant. Exotic locations became part of their normal life as Mrs. Hoover and her two young sons followed her husband to Australia, Japan, Egypt, India, Burma, Russia, and England.

The Hoovers later wrote that those had been days of high adventure. They looked forward to their stay in China and prepared for it by reading everything about the Orient that they could lay their hands on. Several months after their arrival, the outbreak of the Boxer Rebellion amply satisfied their craving for excitement. When the rebellion was over, they began to write a book concerning the background of the Boxer movement and their experiences during the siege of Tientsin, but business pressures and other projects and adventures intervened. Although they later attempted to revive the project as a commentary on Chinese society and customs, neither book was ever completed.[7]

Lou Henry Hoover's life was much fuller than the mere sum of its parts. Reviewing isolated episodes produces only a general idea of the way in which Mrs. Hoover's interests in education, public service, and recreation were blended together in the extraordinary life of a unique first lady. Biographers and historians will eventually provide us with a more complete picture, but a few tentative observations seem in order, especially with regard to potential areas of research and Mrs. Hoover's place within the larger scope of women's history.

Several research possibilities immediately come to mind. One of the more obvious involves her role as first lady. Important changes have taken place over the years in the role of first ladies. Mrs. Hoover's guests appreciated the little touches she added to make them more at ease and welcomed her modification of some aspects of White House protocol.

While she was interested in painting, sculpture, and dance, she seems to have taken a greater interest in music. Her musicales were noted for their richness and variety, and she especially encouraged the appearance of American artists such as Lewis Richards, Rosa Ponselle, Mildred Dilling, and Lawrence Tibbett in addition to such international celebrities as Paderweski, Heifitz, and Horowitz.

Thus her activities as first lady will be of interest to historians regardless of whether they are interested in White House social functions and customs, the role of first ladies as patrons of the arts, or their continuing struggle to carry on with their private lives while living in the goldfish bowl of public life.

One of Mrs. Hoover's projects as first lady resulted in the compilation of a comprehensive history of the traditions and furnishings of the White House. Frustrated by the staff's inability to answer her questions about the great old house, Mrs. Hoover and one of her secretaries conducted extensive research and secured several contributions and gifts of appropriate furnishings. While most of the furnishings from earlier administrations had long since disappeared as one presidential household gave way to the next, many remaining pieces could be identified. President Monroe, the first president to occupy the White House after it had been burned by the British during the War of 1812, had supplied elegant furniture that he had purchased while minister to France. In 1932 Mrs. Hoover secured the permission of Monroe's descendants to make exact copies for the White House. Included in the furnishings for the Monroe Room were several formal pieces and a copy of the desk at which the Monroe Doctrine was written.

Another research possibility concerns Mrs. Hoover's experiences in China. The drafts of the unpublished books on China afford a personal insight into Chinese society at a critical point in that nation's history. Along with her other speeches and writings they provide evidence of her intellectual capacity and interests.

Both the Girl Scouts and the Women's Division of the National Amateur Athletic Federation (NAAF) experienced important changes in the thrusts of their programs in the 1920s and 1930s. Mrs. Hoover's files on these organizations

Newly elected president of the Girl Scouts of America, Lou buys a box of cookies to open the 1935 fund drive. Today, she is best known for her contribution to that movement.

offer a unique vantage point from which to view the changing roles of women and girls in these decades. The debate over the types of sporting events appropriate for women and girls continues unabated—over sixty years after the NAAF entered the discussion. Many other concerns of vital interest to women were being aired during the twenties and thirties, and some of them are reflected in Mrs. Hoover's writings and correspondence.

One historian has already stated that there is "clear evidence of Mrs. Hoover's significant connection to the central issues of women's history for her time," and that "more than any other member of the group" of early twentieth-century first ladies, Mrs. Hoover's life "seemed to dramatize all the exciting possibilities facing the women of her class and generation."[8] Lou Henry Hoover was born at the height of the Victorian period, but her modern attitudes and outlook on life suggest that she was a "transitional woman" whose place in women's history has yet to be defined. Well traveled, articulate, and well read, she lived life to the fullest. Her friend and eulogist Ray Lyman Wilbur obviously had this in mind when he stated that "there is no finer example of how to live than was given us by Lou Henry Hoover."[9] Historians and biographers who study her papers will discover a woman who was in many ways ahead of her time and whose writings and papers add new perspectives on the concerns of her day.

NOTES

[1]Lou Henry Hoover to Jackson Reynolds, Nov. 24, 1914, "Reynolds, Jackson," Personal jCorrespondence Series, Lou Henry Hoover Papers, Herbert Hoover Library, West Branch, IA.

[2]Lou Henry Hoover to Evelyn Wight Allen, n.d., Evelyn Wight Allen Papers, HH Library.

[3]Lou Henry Hoover to Frank B. Kellogg, Mar. 1, 1922, "Kellogg, Frank B.," Personal Correspondence Series, LHH Papers, HH Library.

[4]Lou Henry Hoover to Florence Henry, Aug. 1899, "Henry Family Correspondence," Personal Correspondence Series, LHH Papers, HH Library.

[5]Herbert Hoover, *Memoirs*, vol. 1, *Years of Adventure, 1874–1920* (1951), pp. 141–145.

[6]Lou Henry Hoover, address to Girl Scout conference, c. 1926, quoted in Girl Scouts of the U.S.A., *Lou Henry Hoover: A Tribute from the Girls Scouts* (c. 1944), p. 7.

[7]Portions of Herbert Hoover's account of the siege of Tientsin, which are in Mrs. Hoover's papers, are printed in Tom Walsh, "Herbert Hoover and the Boxer Rebellion," *Prologue* 19(1987):34–40.

[8]Stephanie Cherry-Hoffman, "Lou Henry Hoover: The Life of a Dynamic American Woman," *The American Road* 10(Summer 1985):4.

[9]Ray Lyman Wilbur, Jan. 14, 1944, eulogy delivered at memorial service for Lou Henry Hoover.

"I Want You to Write to Me"

The Papers of Anna Eleanor Roosevelt

By Frances M. Seeber

The team that set a standard for activism: Eleanor Roosevelt with her secretaries Malvina Thompson and Edith Helm.

In August 1933 Mrs. Franklin D. Roosevelt wrote a short article for her page in *Woman's Home Companion.* It was titled simply: "I Want You to Write to Me." Explaining why she issued such an invitation, she said,

> "whatever happens to us in our lives, we find questions constantly recurring that we would gladly discuss with some friend. Yet it is hard to find just the friend we should like to talk to. Often it is easier *to write* to someone whom we do not expect ever to see.[1]

So it was with Eleanor Roosevelt. She touched the American people, and they in turn touched her. Her invitation triggered an avalanche!

Mrs. Roosevelt once quoted the following statistics concerning the mail she received as first lady: "300,000 pieces in 1933, 90,000 in 1937, and about 150,000 in 1940."[2] She was quick to point out that this correspondence did not include the president's mail. Frequently, however, people did write the first lady and asked her to give their messages to the president. One correspondent wrote, "I know you can buttonhole him at breakfast and make him listen." Mrs. Roosevelt responded with good humor, "He would be at breakfast all day and far into the night if he even scanned my mail!"[3] But many citizens felt that she could make the president listen, and in some cases, if he would not do something, she would. In 1941 a black mother wrote to the president complaining about racial discrimination against her son. She concluded with this postscript: "I expect to hear from you right away because if I don't, I'll write to Mrs. Roosevelt!"[4]

The huge amount of mail Mrs. Roosevelt received in those early days prompted her staff to consult the records of previous administrations. To their astonishment they found no comparison between the number of letters Mrs. Roosevelt was receiving and the number addressed to her predecessors. Eleanor Roosevelt attributed the great volume of her mail to the following reasons: first, radio made people more aware of issues and names and encouraged them to write letters; second, the conditions in 1932 and 1933 were such that people were desperate and turned to their government for help; and third, she said people wrote to her because to them she was a symbol.[5]

When Eleanor Roosevelt moved into the White House, she tried to determine what had been the previous custom for answering mail addressed to the president's wife. A pile of form letters was brought to her that was intended to cover every contingency. Some of these letters dated as far back as the Cleveland administration. For example, if a woman wrote and said her child pined for an elephant and would Mrs. [president's wife] provide one, the standard reply under the "form" system would automatically be: "Mrs. [president's wife] has had so many similar requests she deeply regrets she cannot comply with yours!"[6] Mrs. Roosevelt did not believe this form system was adequate to reply to the grave questions asked in the 1930s. She quickly discarded most of the old forms and immediately began to set a new system into motion, one that proved to be highly successful.

The papers of Anna Eleanor Roosevelt at the Franklin D. Roosevelt Library in Hyde Park constitute the second largest collection of materials there and number roughly two million pages. While the early materials are rather fragmented, the so-called "White House" papers, about 490 cubic feet, fully document Mrs. Roosevelt's public and private life. The papers are arranged numerically by file number and thereunder chronologically and alphabetically. A list of major files precedes the inventory. From the researcher's standpoint, the two most important series, or files, from the White House years are "Series 70. Correspondence with Government Departments" and "Series 100. Personal Letters."

The files in Series 70 consist largely of correspondence from the general public. Tens of thousands of citizens wrote to Mrs. Roosevelt for assistance,

First Lady Eleanor Roosevelt autographs caps for sailors stationed on the Galapagos Islands, March 1944. Mrs. Roosevelt's graciousness endeared her to millions.

intercession, or advice. The files of the 1930s reflect the plight of many desperate persons hit by the depression: farmers whose properties were foreclosed; veterans of World War I seeking bonuses, medical help, or hospitalization; unemployed persons appealing for jobs or funds; and families in legal, social, or financial difficulties of every description. These requests led Mrs. Roosevelt to write in 1940, "I think I have been asked to do something about everything in the world except change the weather!"[7] She elaborated on this statement with the following: "A woman wrote and asked me to find a baby for her to adopt. Her second letter explained that if I found the baby, she would need a cow, and if she had the cow, she would need an electric icebox in which to keep the milk for the baby!"[8]

Until the appropriate government agencies were established, Mrs. Roosevelt sent many of the heartrending letters she received to various friends who were in positions to be of help. Later she forwarded the letters to the agencies. She was critical, however, of the fact that so many of her correspondents were not aware of the existence of the agencies that were equipped to help them. "I do not think we have done a very good job in publicizing the various functions of the government agencies, because people write me, and we find the address of the nearest place for them to apply, and often it is practically around the corner from where they live."[9]

Losing one's home was one of the great worries of the middle class in the 1930s. Incoming letters concerning this matter were turned over to the newly formed Home Owner's Loan Corporation (HOLC), and for many this agency was truly a savior as the following letter poignantly demonstrates.

> Dear Mrs. Roosevelt: Thank you very much for helping me to keep my house. If it wasn't for you I know I would have lost it. . . . I would have killed myself if I would have lost my house. I will never forget you. . . . I went to the Home Loan and they said everything would be all right. Forgive me if I caused you any trouble.[10]

Many proud but frightened people were embarrassed by their situations and the fact that they needed help. They, too, wrote to Mrs. Roosevelt but asked that their pleas be kept confidential, and they were. "It is very humiliating for me to have to write you . . ." wrote one, and another declared, "*Please* Mrs. Roosevelt, I do not want charity, only a chance . . . somehow we will manage—but without charity." The latter writer was a young mother with several children. She sent Mrs. Roosevelt two rings "my dearest possessions," she wrote, "to keep as security. . . . If you will consider buying the baby clothes [she sent a list of items she needed], please keep them [the rings] until I send you the money you spent."[11]

Files from after 1940 reflect the general improvement of business conditions, and Mrs. Roosevelt's correspondence begins to deal with aspects of selective service, conditions in military camps, and complaints about the treatment of draftees. As the war advanced, the correspondence reflects the pressures of wartime, appeals from parents for release of their sons from the armed forces, complaints about gas rationing, price controls, race riots, and shortages of goods and services.

A rather small but important series concerning wartime matters in Mrs.

Roosevelt's papers is called "Letters from Servicemen, 1942–1945." It contains approximately sixteen thousand pages. This group of letters is an excellent social and historical commentary on the lives of the men and women in the service and describes the effect of war not only on them but on their families.

Among the many problems faced by servicemen was racial discrimination. It not only disturbed Mrs. Roosevelt but frustrated her as well. She wrote to her friend Joe Lash in 1942,

> Young Neil Vanderbilt (no longer so young) came to see me this p.m. and told me some shocking things about the attitude of officers towards the negro troops. I don't wonder they are resentful & will of course tell FDR but I wonder if he can do anything.[12]

Discrimination against black soldiers was also common outside the service. A young black army private awaiting assignment visited Washington, D.C., in January 1943. His letter to Mrs. Roosevelt recounted his experience. Apparently, during his visit he had stopped at a People's Drug Store where at first he was refused service at the counter, but later was served his drink in a paper cup while a white man sitting next to him received his soda in a glass. For four pages he castigated Mrs. Roosevelt. He informed her that he had four brothers in the service,

> but, as to what they are fighting for God only knows. I'm going to feel fine, fighting in a Jim Crow Army, for a Jim Crow Government . . . and when I might see a white boy dying on a battlefield, I hope to God I won't remember People's Drug Store on January 11th. . . . This is just to let you know how one negro soldier feel [*sic*] going into the service.

In frustration and anger, he added a postscript to the letter: "Here is the cup, to [*sic*] bad some negro boy couldn't give a dying [white] boy a cooling drink on a battlefield." The paper cup is still attached to the correspondence.

Mrs. Roosevelt dictated this signed response several days later. It was sympathetic yet practical.

> I can quite understand how what happened to you made you feel as bitterly as you do feel. There are many things of that kind which many of us in this country deeply regret. The only thing I can say to you is that under the Germans or the Japanese you would have very little freedom, and you certainly would not have the freedom to write to me as you have. You are free to go on working as a people for the betterment of your people and you are gradually gathering behind you a larger and larger group of white people who are conscious of the wrongs and who are helping to correct them.[13]

Whenever possible, most incoming letters in Series 70 were referred to the appropriate governmental agencies for action. If they were not, the reply was drafted by members of Mrs. Roosevelt's staff, usually Malvina Thompson, her private secretary, or Mrs. James Helm, her social secretary. Mrs. Roosevelt replied to relatively few letters in this series, but she did carry on an extensive correspondence about matters brought to her attention by the public with department heads and federal officials, including all the members of the president's cabinet.

Another of Eleanor Roosevelt's admirers and correspondents was England's Prime Minister Winston Churchill. Here they meet during the Quebec Conference, September 1944.

Series 100. Personal Letters, the second of the important files for researchers, may be considered Mrs. Roosevelt's personal file since she drafted and signed about 90 percent of the replies. The material contained in this file reflects and documents Eleanor Roosevelt's interest and service in the fields of labor, the youth movement, civil liberties, public welfare, education, refugee assistance, women's rights, and national defense. A statement in Mrs. Roosevelt's autobiography sheds light on the relationship her correspondence had with the choice of the causes and concerns she made her own.

> . . . my interest or sympathy or indignation is not aroused by an abstract cause but by the plight of a single person. . . . Out of my response to an individual develops an awareness of a problem to the community, then to the country, and finally to the world. In each case my feeling of obligation to do something stemmed from one individual and then widened and became applied to a broader area.[14]

In many of these so called "Personal Letters" Mrs. Roosevelt gave of herself emotionally even to distant correspondents who somehow sensed her willingness to listen to their needs. People wrote to her because they knew that she cared, and in this caring she found an outlet for her own powerful emotional needs. Over and over again Mrs. Roosevelt would answer pleas for help with a sympathetic letter, an admonition to a federal department to take some action, or even a personal check.[15] These personal letters are indispensable to prospective biographers as well as to general historians of the New Deal period because the correspondence demonstrates Eleanor Roosevelt's association with hundreds of experts and leaders in and out of government. Some of her correspondents included black educator Mary McLeod Bethune, novelist Pearl Buck, Madame Chiang Kai-Shek, Prime Minister Winston Churchill, Congresswoman and friend Helen Gahagan Douglas, philanthropist Mary Lasker, Secretary of the Treasury Henry Morgenthau, Jr., Congresswoman Caroline O'Day, Secretary of Labor Frances Perkins, Walter Reuther of the UAW, welfare expert Lillian Wald, and Walter White of the NAACP.

Extensive and enlightening exchanges took place between Mrs. Roosevelt and her family and old friends. One of the latter was Carola von Schaffer-Bernstein, a school chum from their Allenswood days in England. Carola was a Berliner, and her pro-Hitler stand in the early days of World War II prompted a sharp reply to one of her letters in 1939. Mrs. Roosevelt wrote:

> Although we do not hate the German people, there is only an inability here to understand how people of spirit can be terrified by one man and his storm troops to the point of countenancing the kind of horrors which seem to have come on in Germany not only where the Jews are concerned, but in the case of the Catholics and some of the liberal German Protestants. . . .
>
> I hope that we are not facing another four years of struggle and I hope that our country will not have to go to war, but no country can exist free and unoppressed while a man like Hitler remains in power.[16]

Eleanor Roosevelt has been described as the "first media first lady."[17] Mrs. Roosevelt was a friend of the press, especially the women of the press. She not only gave these women status and opportunities they had not been afforded in the past, but she also enlisted them in her causes. She encouraged these press women to pass on to her their impressions of who and what they saw, here and abroad. There is much exciting material from news correspondents and reporters in this series including exchanges from Lorena Hickok on politics and relief activities across the country in the 1930s, correspondence from Ruby Black describing the economic conditions and politics of Puerto Rico, letters from Martha Gellhorn Hemingway on the Spanish Civil War and the plight of refugees, reports from Anna Louise Strong during and after her visits to Russia and China, and material from war correspondent Doris Fleeson concerning Mrs. Roosevelt's wartime trips to Australia and the Pacific. Much of their correspondence is located in Series 100. Personal Letters, but an unofficial organization of some of these women journalists became known as Mrs. Roosevelt's Press Conference Association. The papers of this group have been deposited at the Roosevelt Library.

One of Eleanor Roosevelt's enduring legacies to her successors in the White House was the life she built for herself when she was on her own after FDR's death. To reporters who met her at Pennsylvania Station in April 1945 when she returned to New York, she said simply, "The story is over." But of course, it was not over; it was just beginning. In the last seventeen years of her life, Mrs. Roosevelt finally came into her own. She emerged from the confusion of her widowhood and created a new career for herself. Instead of retreating into private life, she became a public figure in her own right and went on to become the acknowledged "First Lady of the World," a title bestowed on her by President Harry S. Truman.

A large portion of Mrs. Roosevelt's post-White House correspondence, 1945–62, consists of letters from the general public, although there are many letters from personal friends, acquaintances, relatives, and associates. The files reflect her myriad activities during these years. A considerable amount of correspondence for each year consists of tributes to and criticisms of President Roosevelt; requests for photographs, autographs, stamps, franked envelopes, material assistance, employment, interviews and advice, statements, endorsements, and contributions; invitations to speak and to attend dinners and meetings; and requests to write books and articles as well as prefaces and introductions for other authors. The material includes a large number of public reaction letters to Mrs. Roosevelt's "My Day" columns. In 1949 there were numerous letters (about six thousand) responding to her controversy with Cardinal Spellman of New York over public aid to parochial schools and, in 1957, on her trip to the Soviet Union.

Although much of the material is routine, it is interesting to discover that Mrs. Roosevelt at times wrote significant responses on both domestic and international issues to ordinary citizens. An example of this is a letter she wrote to Mrs. Hugh N. Marshall of Dayton, Oregon, in December 1950. At this time, Mrs. Roosevelt was the United States' delegate to the United Nations. In her letter Mrs. Roosevelt defends FDR's Russian policy; denies being a Communist;

Eleanor Roosevelt found her work with the United Nations the most satisfying in her long and marked career, particularly her role in the struggle for the adoption of the Universal Declaration of Human Rights in 1949.

denies FDR was a protégé of Gerhart Eisler; denies Joe Lash is a protégé of hers; declares her support for Helen Gahagan Douglas; denies Melvyn Douglas is a Communist; defends Dean Acheson; says Alger Hiss was convicted of perjury on circumstantial evidence, not of being a Communist; and implies that Fulton Lewis, Westbrook Pegler, and John O'Donnell are not "decent" people![18] All this is contained in a two-page dictated, but signed, letter.

Other topics she addressed during the post-White House years were those of public concern. For the years immediately after World War II, there is much correspondence relating to the problems of refugees and displaced persons, American relief efforts, the United Nations, and American foreign policy. There is also correspondence concerning domestic politics, communism, the McCarthy hearings, presidential campaigns, racial integration, and school desegregation. Minority rights is a recurring theme throughout the correspondence, and there are some letters from almost every year concerning the plight of blacks, American Indians, and women. Except for the years 1945–48, the material in Mrs. Roosevelt's papers is arranged chronologically by year and thereunder in very rough and sometimes unreliable alphabetical order by name of correspondent or organization. Material for 1945–48 has been merged into a single bloc and is arranged alphabetically.

Although Mrs. Roosevelt's post-White House papers consist principally of incoming and outgoing correspondence, they also include memorandums, reports, programs, drafts of speeches, articles, clippings, printed material, and copies of her famous "My Day" columns. These columns, which were begun on December 31, 1935, and continued until September 26, 1962, little more than a month before she died, represent the only consistent day-to-day diary Eleanor Roosevelt kept. Regrettably, only a very small portion of the collected columns is indexed.

In the 1930s and 1940s, Mrs. Roosevelt wrote monthly columns for such magazines as *Woman's Home Companion, Ladies Home Journal*, and *McCall's*. In these she replied to readers' questions and often revealed a side of herself not often seen elsewhere by stating her philosophy of life in a simple, homey way. Not a few questions, however, were obviously sent to the first lady by members of the administration in order to explain, advocate, or make public certain issues or points of view.

Several ancillary collections at the Roosevelt Library complement and complete Mrs. Roosevelt's own papers since they contain a fair amount of Eleanor Roosevelt's correspondence. The papers of Anna Roosevelt Halsted, the only daughter of President and Mrs. Roosevelt, contain over eight hundred handwritten letters from her famous mother. The Lorena Hickok Papers; the papers of Marion Dickerman, Hilda Smith, and Molly Dewson; the Roosevelt Family Papers; and the papers of the Women's Division of the National Committee of the Democratic Party all contain Eleanor Roosevelt correspondence that reveals the personality and multifaceted career of this first lady.

The post-White House years brought no respite to Eleanor Roosevelt. She immersed herself in the work of the United Nations and would later confess that her appointment to the U.N. was that part of her life's work of which she was most proud. Especially important to her was the role she played in the struggle for the adoption of the Universal Declaration of Human Rights. Her belief in the human rights of all individuals was the cornerstone of her philosophy of life and is almost thematic in her papers. Each individual mattered to the country and to the world. In a speech on human rights, delivered in 1958, Eleanor Roosevelt said:

> Where, after all, do universal human rights begin? In small places, close to home—so close and so small that they cannot be seen on any maps of the world. Yet they are the world of the individual persons; the neighborhood he lives in; the school or college he attends; the factory, farm, office where he works. Such are the places where every man, woman, and child seeks equal justice, equal opportunity, equal dignity without discrimination. Unless these rights have meaning there, they have little meaning anywhere. Without concerned citizen action to uphold them close to home, we shall look in vain for progress in the larger world.[19]

Mrs. Roosevelt's vision was one of a better world, and this ideal is documented over and over again in her correspondence, speeches, and writings. It was the reason she was often at the heart of change and more often, its source. She believed she could make a difference in this world, and the hundreds of thousands of individuals who wrote to her wanted to believe she could. Whatever the role or nonrole ascribed to Eleanor Roosevelt in twentieth-century American history, it is a fact that no other first lady was so much the center of controversy. No other first lady had her influence. No other so affected the lives of the women who followed her.[20]

Notes

[1]Mrs. Franklin D. Roosevelt, "I Want You to Write to Me," *Woman's Home Companion*, (Aug. 1933): 4.

[2]Eleanor Roosevelt, "Mail of a President's Wife," unpublished article, c. 1939, p. 1, Speech and Article File, 1939, Eleanor Roosevelt Papers, Franklin D. Roosevelt Library, Hyde Park, NY.

[3]"Mrs. Eleanor Roosevelt's Own Radio Program," July 25, 1940, p. 4, Speech and Article File, 1940, ER Papers, FDR Library.

[4]Dorothy I. Height, speech, Oct. 14, 1984, Eleanor Roosevelt Centennial Conference, Vassar College.

[5]Roosevelt, "Mail of a President's Wife," p. 1, Speech and Article File, 1939, ER Papers, FDR Library.

[6]Eleanor Roosevelt, "My Mail," unpublished article, c. 1940, Speech and Article File, 1940, ER Papers, FDR Library.

[7]Roosevelt, "Mail of a President's Wife," p. 2, Speech and Article File, 1939, ER Papers, FDR Library.

[8]Ibid.

[9]Ibid., p. 1.

[10]J. Graziano to Eleanor Roosevelt, Aug. 28, 1934, 70. Correspondence with Government Departments, 1934, Gl–Gu, ER Papers, FDR Library.

[11]R. Trickel to Eleanor Roosevelt, Apr. 3, 1935, 70. 150.1 Material Assistance Requested, 1935, Ti–Wh, and H. Champine to Eleanor Roosevelt, Jan. 2, 1935, 70. Correspondence with Government Departments, 1935, Ch–Co, ER Papers, FDR Library.

[12]Eleanor Roosevelt to Joseph P. Lash, May 1, 1942, Eleanor Roosevelt–Joseph P. Lash Correspondence, May 1942, Joseph P. Lash Papers, FDR Library.

[13]Pvt. Clifton Searles to Eleanor Roosevelt, Jan. 11, 1942 [*sic*], and Eleanor Roosevelt to Searles, Jan. 23, 1943, 100.1 Letters from Servicemen, 1943, P–S, ER Papers, FDR Library.

[14]Eleanor Roosevelt, *Autobiography* (1961), p. 413.

[15]William Chafe, "Biographical Sketch," in Joan Hoff-Wilson and Marjorie Lightman, eds., *Without Precedent: The Life and Career of Eleanor Roosevelt* (1984), p. 18.

[16]Eleanor Roosevelt to Carola von Schaffer-Bernstein, Sept. 6, 1939, 100. Personal Letters, 1939, Bem–Bi, ER Papers, FDR Library.

[17]Abigail McCarthy, "Eleanor Roosevelt as First Lady," in Hoff-Wilson and Lightman, eds., *Without Precedent*, p. 218.

[18]Eleanor Roosevelt to Mrs. Hugh N. Marshall, Dec. 11, 1950, General Correspondence, 1950, Mac–Mez, ER Papers, FDR Library.

[19]Hoff-Wilson and Lightman, eds., *Without Precedent*, p. xix.

[20]Ibid., p. 214.

Harry's Silent Partner

The Papers of Bess Truman

By Maurine H. Beasley

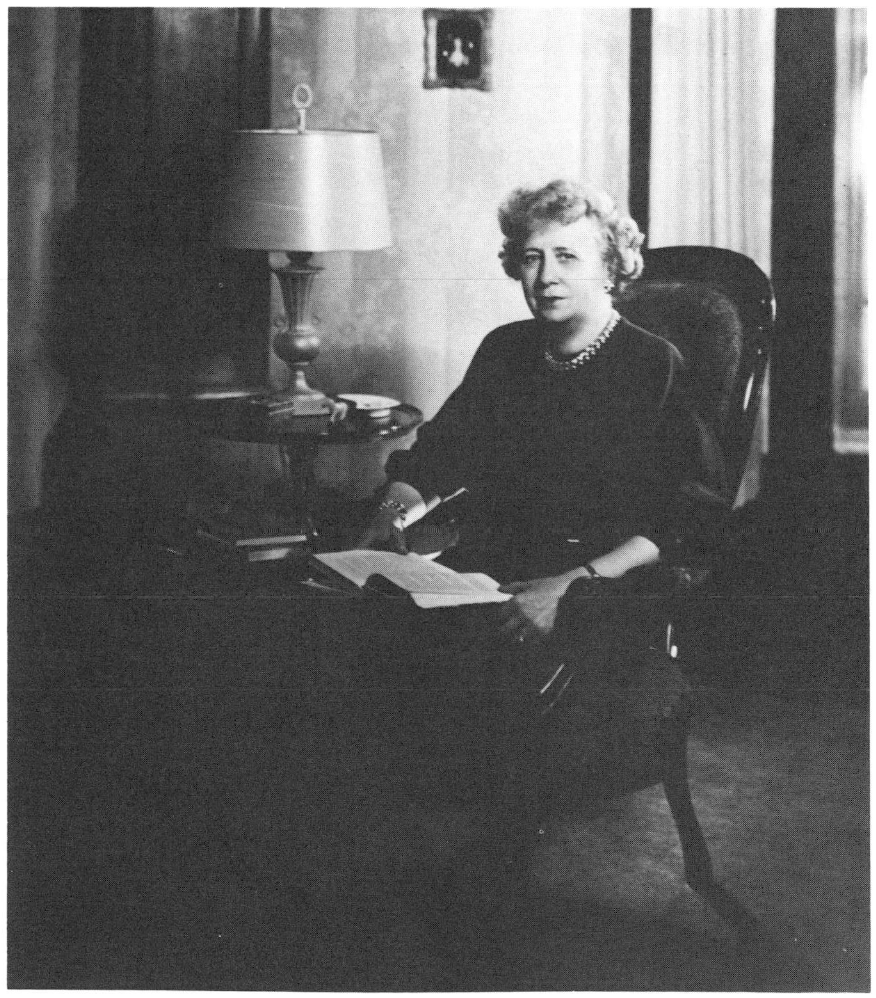

Elizabeth Virginia "Bess" Wallace Truman (1885–1982) at home, 1949. Mrs. Truman held strong convictions and had few reservations about airing them "Missouri-style—straight from the shoulder."

Of all the twentieth-century first ladies, none was more reluctant to act her part than Bess Wallace Truman. Many little girls dream of growing up to live in the White House and serve as a ceremonial figure in the complex symbolism that marks the office of the president of the United States. But for Bess Truman, a down-to-earth, motherly woman who remained firmly rooted in her hometown of Independence, Missouri, the artificial world of Washington politics and power held little appeal. She remained just what she wanted to be: a representative of middle-American values and virtues who happened to preside over the White House due to historical accident. Reared to be a lady by a well-to-do Independence family, she personified traditional ideas regarding a woman's proper sphere.

Yet this does not mean that Bess Truman failed to recognize the importance of her role as first lady or to fulfill it effectively as a political symbol. Although her formal education had ended with a year at a finishing school for young women in Kansas City, Bess Truman possessed a ready wit and a supple mind. The only girl in a family of four children, she was known as the best tennis player in Independence as well as for making top grades during her high school years. Harry S. Truman, to whom she was married at the age of thirty-four after a courtship of almost nine years, referred to her as "The Boss." He obviously valued her counsel and respected her judgment in political and personal matters. In the White House she remained her husband's confidante and trusted adviser, an individual with whom he could share his deepest concerns.

Bess Truman, however, was not one to leave an obvious record of her own importance in the Truman administration. According to her only child, Margaret Truman Daniel, her mother "kept her deepest feelings, her most profound sorrows, sealed from my view—from almost everyone's view."[1] Nevertheless, intriguing hints of Bess Truman's conscious decisions on involvement, or lack of it, in the Truman administration can be found by a careful study of papers located at the Truman Library in Independence, Missouri. While the library has only a small amount of correspondence written by Bess Truman herself, what is there still provides glimpses of her attitude toward the position of first lady and her view of herself in it.

Unlike her predecessor, Eleanor Roosevelt, who had embarked on a public career before her husband's election as president, Bess Truman had remained totally within the domestic sphere before her husband unexpectedly succeeded to the presidency following the death of Franklin D. Roosevelt on April 12, 1945. Though she had done clerical work in Truman's office when he had been U.S. senator from Missouri, she had been on the payroll simply because the Trumans needed her salary to help defray their living costs in Washington.[2] When Mrs. Roosevelt tried to arrange for Mrs. Truman to hold press conferences with Washington women reporters after becoming first lady, a practice that Mrs. Roosevelt had originated in 1933, Mrs. Truman declined to do so.[3]

Mrs. Truman, however, worked hard at the task of being first lady This can be readily gleaned from studying the two main files at the Truman Library that deal with Mrs. Truman's duties as first lady. One is the Office of Social Correspondence file, a record of the official correspondence of Mrs. Truman and her daughter, Margaret, and the other the Records of the White House Social Office, which planned official social events.

Somewhat more enlightening from a personal perspective are the papers of Mary Paxton Keeley, Bess Truman's lifelong friend from Independence who held the distinction of being the first woman graduate of the School of Journalism of the University of Missouri. Other material can be found in the papers of Reathel Odum, personal secretary to Mrs. Truman, and Alonzo Fields, chief butler at the White House during the Truman administration.

Correspondence and memorandums addressed to Mrs. Truman or to members of the White House staff about Mrs. Truman are located in the White House Central Files under the category of the President's Personal File. Also in the White House Central Files may be found the official file pertaining to Mrs. Truman's decision to attend a tea given in her honor on October 12, 1945, by the Daughters of American Revolution in the face of protests by Rep. Adam Clayton Powell, who announced that his wife, pianist Hazel Scott, had been barred from performing in the D.A.R. auditorium, Constitution Hall, because she was black.

In addition, valuable insight into Mrs. Truman's conception of her role as first lady can be gained from research in the Truman Library's audiovisual collection. The collection includes at least one thousand photographs showing the transformation of Bess Truman from a tomboyish adolescent into a conventional-appearing wife and mother and subsequently a rather rigid-looking first lady. The last president's wife to escape extensive coverage on television, Mrs. Truman often found herself the object of newsreel and press photographers who captured her on film as a short, plump woman with grey hair worn in a short, curly style known as a "poodle cut." She was usually shown wearing boxy, tailored suits with hats and gloves to match. She looked, her husband said, "just like a woman ought to look who's been happily married for a quarter of a century."[4]

Mrs. Truman's unwillingness to assume a public stance is conveyed in the one-linear-foot collection of papers of her secretary, Reathel Odum. Although Mrs. Truman refused to hold regular press conferences, she was forced to maintain some contact with Washington women reporters accustomed to the steady flow of news created by Eleanor Roosevelt. Consequently, Mrs. Truman designated Edith Helm, the White House social secretary under the Roosevelts who remained on to help the Trumans, and Odum to conduct weekly press briefings.

Bess Truman welcomes a young visitor suffering from muscular dystrophy to the White House. Although a warmhearted hostess, Mrs. Truman found the lack of privacy discomforting and kept social activities to a minimum during her years as first lady.

The Odum papers contain examples of the kinds of questions the secretaries passed on to Mrs. Truman from women reporters and her terse, often one-word answers. For example:

> Q. What is Mrs. Truman's conception of the role of First Lady? A. No comment.
>
> Q. What qualities, innate or acquired, does she think would be the greatest asset for the wife of a President? For instance, good health, enjoyment of people, knowledge of languages, etc. A. Good health and a well-developed sense of humor.

Beginning in the 1920s, Bess Truman shared public appearances with her husband as was expected of candidates' wives. A happy couple fresh from their victory at the polls in 1948, the Trumans joined the hoopla at the annual Army-Navy game.

> Q. If such a thing were possible—what special training would she recommend to prepare a woman for the role of the First Lady? A. No comment.
>
> Q. Any special professional background? A. Skill in public speaking would be very helpful.
>
> Q. Does she think there ever will be a woman President of the United States? A. No.
>
> Q. Would she want to be President? A. No.[5]

The Odum papers, however, reveal that Mrs. Truman understood the need to keep open channels of communication with reporters in spite of her unwillingness to reveal her own views. They contain copies of mimeographed lists of Mrs. Truman's social engagements, which were passed out to reporters regularly. Often these were covered on the woman's and society pages of the day.

An occasional handwritten memo from Mrs. Truman to Odum gives the flavor of Mrs. Truman's warm personality and down-to-earth common sense in dealing with the press. For instance, Odum informed Mrs. Truman on October 11, 1946, that Betty Beale, a society reporter for the *Washington Star*, had telephoned and asked why Margaret Truman had remained in Independence instead of returning to Washington for a Junior League training course. "Miss Beale insisted that I ask you the reason for Margaret's staying in Missouri," Odum explained. "Finishing a course in voice lessons," Mrs. Truman wrote in reply, adding, "Better tell her. God only knows what they may be saying. I'd prefer telling her it's none of their d— business."[6]

Similar flashes of wit and frankness appear in the small collection of handwritten letters from Mrs. Truman to her childhood friend from Independence, Mary Paxton Keeley. Preserved in the Keeley collection, they portray Mrs. Truman as a forthright individual with a keen grasp of her husband's affairs. Following the Trumans' unexpected elevation to the White House, Mrs. Truman wrote Keeley to thank her for a letter, insisting, "I took time to read it you may bet on that."[7]

Commenting on her husband's succession to the presidency, Mrs. Truman, then sixty years old, wrote, "We are not any of us happy to be where we are but there's nothing to be done about it except to do our best—and forget about the sacrifices and many unpleasant things that bob up."[8] She proceeded to mention one—a rumor that Harry Truman intended to appoint Duke Shoop, the Washington correspondent for the *Kansas City Star*, as his press secretary, even though Shoop previously had written stories critical of the Trumans. "Don't worry about Duke," Mrs. Truman assured her old friend. "He's made an ass of himself the way he broadcast the fact that he was going to be H's Press Sec'y. Even went down to the Press Club & spread it there of all places. If there is anybody on earth that H. has absolutely *no* use for it's D.S."[9]

Mrs. Truman's determination to remain herself—a small-town housewife living temporarily at the seat of Washington power—pervaded a thank-you note to Keeley in 1946 for a homey Christmas gift. "I surely am delighted to have a handmade dish-cloth," Mrs. Truman wrote. "You must have had some sort of a hunch about my stock of dish clothes.—And are they hard to get!—Anyway, ones you can't throw a dog through."[10]

When Keeley wrote Mrs. Truman to compliment Margaret Truman on her singing career, Mrs. Truman's response included her reflections on living in the White House:

> I am so *glad* you heard Marg sing and approved! Of course we were very proud of her—really more because she had nerve enough to do it than of her performance. . . . M. is going back to NY tomorrow & *get to work*. . . . Thank goodness she is really *interested* in *something* & is not content to sit around in Wash for the next two years—It becomes very deadly in a hurry.[11]

Yet not even to Keeley did Mrs. Truman use language that departed from the Victorian ideal of ladylike conduct. When Keeley advised her to not attend the D.A.R. tea in the face of the protest from Rep. Adam Clayton Powell, Mrs. Truman replied, "I agree with you that the DAR is dynamite at present and I'm not 'having any' just now. But I was plenty burned up with the wire I had from that _______ in NY."[12] Rather than use an unseemly word, Mrs. Truman left a blank space in the letter.

She also attended the tea, although she was not a segregationist, according to her daughter. Margaret Truman has since written that her mother refused at the time to recognize that she was a public figure and was determined not to let a congressman control her social activities.[13] Her presence at the tea set her in sharp contrast to Eleanor Roosevelt, who had resigned from the D.A.R. in 1939 after a black singer, Marian Anderson, had been denied the right to perform at Constitution Hall. The official file of mail received by the White House on the controversy, located in the White House Central Files, shows a fairly even split on the issue, manifesting the racial climate of the times.

The hard work that Mrs. Truman did as first lady is documented in the five linear feet of Office of Social Correspondence files and the twenty-five linear feet of files of the White House Social Office. While almost none of the material is in Mrs. Truman's handwriting, these voluminous records detail the efforts of one of the busiest White House hostesses. In the fall of 1946 Mrs. Truman reinstituted the formal White House social season, which had been interrupted by World War II, and oversaw arrangements for a myriad of events ranging from formal state receptions to teas and musicales.

In addition, Mrs. Truman made hundreds of public appearances to promote various causes. She lent her prestige to scores of charitable, patriotic, and civic organizations, serving as an honorary member, patron, or sponsor in connection with benevolent events. She acted as honorary president of the Girl Scouts and the Women's National Democratic Club. As an honorary member of the American Newspaper Women's Club she attended functions of this group, which was started by writers for society pages. Although correspondence with organizations was typed by her secretarial staff, Mrs. Truman meticulously answered mail personally and signed thank-you notes. A typical example from the Social Office files is a letter dated January 20, 1950, to the president of the American Newspaper Women's Club, Margaret Hart Canby: "Looking around the room at your party last Tuesday, it seemed to me that, like ourselves, everyone was having loads of fun. It is a marvel to me how you girls in the American Newspaper Women's Club manage to think up so many new and original ideas."[14]

The files contain occasional evidence of the dislike of Mrs. Truman, a product of Victorian restraint, for the incessant socializing she was called upon to do. For instance, Mrs. Truman scrawled a question on a letter from the president of the National League of American Pen Women complaining that the first lady had canceled a tentative acceptance to attend a breakfast meeting. "Can I get by doing this?" Mrs. Truman wrote, marking a passage in the letter in which the president implored her to at least receive delegates to the organization's convention.[15]

Mrs. Truman's strong hand in overseeing food service at the White House is manifest in the papers of Alonzo Fields, the White House's chief butler. The collection includes examples of menus approved by the first lady with comments from Fields. In one case he noted that Mrs. Truman rejected three menus proposed for a ladies' luncheon on February 8, 1952, but agreed to accept one for a luncheon on February 19, "so this day was not a total loss."[16] The menu finally approved was for curried shrimp in a rice ring.

Items pertaining to Mrs. Truman in the President's Personal File offer considerable insight into the social history of the Truman era. It contains copies of thousands of requests to Mrs. Truman for help. Ranging from the pathetic to the ridiculous, the letters seek aid for personal difficulties including poverty, unemployment, imprisonment, collection of pensions, injuries, and illnesses. Many letters came from citizens of other countries asking for food, medical help, and emergency assistance, reflecting the chaotic conditions in Europe after World War II. Letter writers were sent standard answers noting that their letters had been referred to appropriate government agencies for replies.

In summary, the papers pertaining to Mrs. Truman at the Truman Library suggest that she made a definite decision not to follow in the footsteps of her predecessor. Rather than trying to be what she was not—a political activist who felt at home in the public arena—Mrs. Truman determinedly limited her horizons. Yet in spite of her refusals to be quoted or to hold press conferences, Mrs. Truman showed skill in her dealings with the press because she maintained contacts with women reporters and provided them with structured news of her activities.

Letters from some members of the public indicate that she was admired for being different from Eleanor Roosevelt. "You are a Greater First Lady in every way, than Eleanor Roosevelt ever thought of being, and much more to be admired," wrote a Pennsylvania woman who applauded Mrs. Truman's decision to attend the controversial D.A.R. tea.[17] Other correspondents disagreed. But by the time Bess Truman left the White House in 1952 she had won respect for conducting herself with dignity and graciousness. If her monosyllabic answers to almost all questions forced the press to present her as a stereotypical wife and mother, perhaps this was the way Americans of the post-World War II period wanted to see their first lady. Indeed, the records indicate that Mrs. Truman may have made a wise political decision to remain a silent partner in the Truman administration as far as public communication was concerned.

Without doubt, Mrs. Truman did serve as a political asset to her husband. Her personal warmth was conveyed in handwritten notes to old acquaintances like this one to Summerfield Jones of West Plains, Missouri: "It was a very real pleasure to give your birthday card to my husband. It means a great deal to us to have these good wishes from our friends."[18]

In hand-signed letters to multitudes of groups that visited the White House, Mrs. Truman exhibited the charm that drew individuals to her. A typical example was this one to Edna H. Barr of the Washington Pan-Hellenic Council:

> One of the pleasantest teas that I have ever had was the one yesterday when the members of the Washington Pan-Hellenic Council came here. It was a pleasure to meet so many agreeable women and I hope that you will extend my warm thanks to them for the exquisite corsage of orchids which they sent to me.[19]

Because of her manner and bearing, Mrs. Truman drew almost no criticism of her performance as first lady except for the D.A.R. tea incident. This is apparent from an examination of press clippings about her contained in a vertical file at the Truman Library. As one who turned down numerous opportunities to contribute articles to various publications that would have paid her well, Mrs. Truman was seen as a genuine individual without desire to profit from her husband's office.

Even Sen. Joseph R. McCarthy, the Communist-hunting Republican from Wisconsin who tore into the Truman administration, found Mrs. Truman an

Mrs. Truman supported the work of the Girl Scouts and its commitment to health and character. As a child, she was herself "a marvelous athelete—the best third baseman in Independence, a superb tennis player, a tireless ice skater."

exemplary first lady. When Mrs. Truman's name surfaced in a Senate inquiry into alleged "influence peddlers" in the administration, McCarthy came to her rescue and absolved her of blame in accepting a deep-freeze unit from Maj. Gen. Harry H. Vaughan, President Truman's military aide.

"I am sure that she did not know anything about this matter. She just graciously accepted a gift and knew nothing of the background," a press clipping in the file quotes McCarthy as saying. "She is the type of lady who is incapable of doing anything improper."[20]

It was in this same spirit that millions of Americans appreciated Bess W. Truman's performance as first lady. She personified the continuation of a durable tradition in American political life: the ideal companion for a president presenting herself as an honest, friendly, and warm individual who acts as a mother figure for the nation. If she did it at the price of subordinating her own preferences and personality, she simply responded to the training and expectations for genteel women of her period. By refusing to accept elements of a public role that she did not want, she in a sense upheld the right of women, even first ladies, to maintain their personal integrity as they saw it. Rather than attempt unsuccessfully to be a copy of Mrs. Roosevelt, Mrs. Truman held to her own tightly disciplined personality. A study of her papers tells the story not only of her but of middle-class women in general in mid-twentieth-century America.

Notes

[1]Margaret Truman, "A Word to the Reader," *Bess W. Truman* (1986).

[2]Quoted by Hugh Fulton in Jhan Robbins, *Bess & Harry: An American Love Story* (1980), p. 70.

[3]Oral history interview with Frances Perkins, Columbia University Oral History Project, as quoted in Gerry Van de Heuvel, "Remembering Bess," *Washington Post*, Oct. 29, 1982, p. D11.

[4]Quoted in Robbins, *Bess & Harry*, p. 99.

[5]Dorothy Williams and Martha Kearney to Reathel Odum, Aug. 29, 1947, box 5, Odum Papers, Harry S. Truman Library, Independence, Mo. See also "Behind Mrs. Truman's Social Curtain: No Comment," *Newsweek*, Nov. 10, 1947, p. 16.

[6]Reathel Odum to Mrs. Truman, Oct. 11, 1946, with answer, box 4, Odum Papers, HST Library.

[7]Bess Truman to Mary Paxton Keeley, May 12, 1945, box 1, Keeley Papers, HST Library.

[8]Ibid.

[9]Ibid.

[10]Bess Truman to Mary Paxton Keeley, Jan. 8, 1946, box 1, Keeley Papers, HST Library.

[11]Bess Truman to Mary Paxton Keeley, Apr. 4, 1947, box 1, Keeley Papers, HST Library.

[12]Bess Truman to Mary Paxton Keeley, 1945, box 1, Keeley Papers, HST Library.

[13]Truman, *Bess W. Truman*, p. 279.

[14]Bess W. Truman to Margaret Hart Canby, Jan. 20, 1950, box 1, White House Social Office Files, HST Library.

[15]Margaret H. Sebree to Edith Helm, Nov. 1, 1949, box 15, White House Social Office Files, HST Library.

[16]Comments accompanying menu for Feb. 19, 1952, box 1, Alonzo Fields Papers, HST Library.

[17]Elizabeth Burnette to Mrs. Harry S. Truman, Oct. 12, 1945, box 124, White House Social Correspondence File, HST Library.

[18]Bess W. Truman to Summerfield Jones, May 12, 1945, box 12, White House Social Office Files, HST Library.

[19]Bess W. Truman to Edna H. Barr, Nov. 6, 1947, box 44, Social Function File, Records of the White House Social Office, HST Library.

[20]H. Walton Cloke, "Senate Republican Says Mrs. Truman Is in Clear on Gift," *New York Times*, Aug. 16, 1949, Vertical File on Bess W. Truman, HST Library.

Ike Was Her Career

The Papers of Mamie Doud Eisenhower

By *Martin M. Teasley*

Mamie Doud Eisenhower's bangs and winsome smile became trademarks of this popular first lady.

Mamie Doud Eisenhower first entered the public limelight in 1942 when her husband, Lt. Gen. Dwight D. Eisenhower, was appointed Supreme Commander of U.S. forces in the European Theater during World War II. On that occasion, a society reporter for the *Washington Post* wrote an article entitled "Presenting: Mrs. Eisenhower." The piece on Mamie opened with the statement, "SHE'S A CAREER WOMAN. Her career is 'Ike.' "[1] This fact remained true throughout her fifty-two years of marriage. Ike was Mamie's career, from her early years as the wife of a company grade officer through her eight years as one of America's most popular first ladies.

The Mamie Doud Eisenhower Papers at the Eisenhower Library provide insight into the special role Mamie played as the wife of one of the important military and political figures in twentieth-century American history. Library holdings contain over one million pages of MDE material, including personal letters, official correspondence, and public mail. The most important papers are located in three series that document her views, her personality, and the role she played while Eisenhower served successively as president of Columbia University (1948–50), as the first NATO commander (1951–52), and as thirty-fourth president of the United States (1953–61).

The Columbia University Series of the Mamie Doud Eisenhower Papers totals some twenty-four hundred pages and is the earliest substantial documentation available on Mamie's public role. The series is divided into two subseries, "Personal Correspondence" and "Household Files," each arranged alphabetically. The SHAPE Series covers the period 1951–52 in Paris when Ike served as head of the Supreme Headquarters, Allied Powers Europe. The SHAPE Series is also arranged alphabetically and totals two thousand pages. Most important is the White House Series, which contains over forty thousand pages. This alphabetically arranged series consists of personal correspondence between Mrs. Eisenhower and close personal friends and family members during her years as first lady.

Mamie viewed as her foremost official duty that of being the best hostess possible. She was better prepared for this challenge than almost any other first lady, before or since. While Ike was NATO commander there was not a royal family or European head of government she had not met or entertained.[2] As the wife of a senior military officer, protocol was a way of life for her.

At the same time, Mamie was a master of sincere small talk. White House Chief Usher J. B. West noted that to every lady who passed by the receiving line at official functions she had something to say: "I love your earrings" or "What state are you from?"—"Oh, yes, I bought a beautiful shawl in Idaho."[3]

Numerous written accolades for her personal charm are located throughout Mamie's White House files. Katherine Howard, deputy administrator of the Federal Civil Defense Administration, thanked Mamie for the special tour given to the Civil Defense National Women's Advisory Council and noted that the group was "enchanted" with the first lady. "They all spoke of your warmth, your youthfulness, your unhurried hospitality."[4] Mrs. Earl Warren wrote Mamie after one of her visits to the White House, "How I envy your ability to convey to others the feeling that you are genuinely pleased to meet them without ever showing any of the strain which must necessarily come from long hours of entertaining."[5]

And strain there was. Mamie wrote to her Denver friend, Mrs. Aksel Nielson, that "April and May (1953) have been my two hardest months. I have asked Mrs. McCaffree today to count up the many hands I have shaken for the last six or eight weeks. After yesterday's 1300, Friday's 3000, Thursday's 1200, the right member is a little weak!"[6]

Mamie's health limited her ability to carry out her official role. She had a rheumatic heart and avoided unnecessary strain. Her health fears were not unfounded since one sister had died of a heart condition and another was a diabetic semi-invalid. She held morning staff consultations from her bed and, to conserve her strength, scheduled her duties in short time-blocks in the afternoon whenever possible.[7]

Mamie's ability to charm as a White House hostess was matched by her thoughtfulness as a correspondent with the public and friends. As the president-elect's wife in late November 1952, she wrote Gen. Alfred Gruenther, a family friend and successor to Ike at NATO, that despite having seven secretaries working on her letters, with no sign of let-up in the volume, she was nevertheless "determined to answer each one in a personal way."[8]

Mamie continued this practice throughout the Eisenhower presidency, even attempting to personally answer the thousands of letters of concern she received from the public during Eisenhower's several illnesses. Pat Nixon wrote to Mamie that the neighborhood delicatessen owner reported in great detail about the letter his friend had received from the first lady. "People are marvelling that you have personally signed so much mail, and they are filled with admiration and appreciation."[9]

The White House Social Office records, totaling over five hundred thousand pages, reveal the extent of Mamie's correspondence with the general public. Although the social office records have not yet been processed and opened for research, a "spot review" policy allows researchers to request a quick screening and opening of specific folders listed in the finding aid to the collection.

Mamie Eisenhower and Pat Nixon sport flowery spring hats while attending a luncheon and fashion show in March 1958.

But it was not the mere volume of correspondence Mrs. Eisenhower answered that was impressive. Sen. Stuart Symington observed in a letter to Mamie, "you always write as if you meant it—I suppose that is one of the reasons you have the country in the palm of your hand."[10]

During the retirement years at the Gettysburg farm, Mamie kept up her "pen pal" relationship with the American people. The Eisenhower Library's holdings from the postpresidential period include over five hundred thousand pages of correspondence between the former first lady and the public, not including some seventy thousand sympathy cards and letters of condolence received on the occasion of Ike's death in 1969. Many of her letters were handwritten, and she spent the entire day at the Gettysburg farm answering mail, if necessary. Mamie's philosophy was "If someone buys a card and takes time to write, the least I can do is to thank them."[11]

Mamie Eisenhower ran a "tight ship" in her household, whether it was at the Columbia University president's house on Morningside Drive, the NATO commander's villa in Marnes La Coquette, or 1600 Pennsylvania Avenue. In *Upstairs at the White House*, Chief Usher West reported that she established her "command" immediately. She knew exactly what she wanted and how it should be done. Mamie could give orders as if *she* were the five-star general, and in fact, she was the commander at home. "Ike took care of the office—I ran the house," she always explained.[12]

A revealing incident occurred after only two weeks in the White House when Mamie was shown a menu for a stag luncheon. "What's this?" she asked Mr. West, referring to the notation "Approved DDE." When told that the president had approved the menu, she shook her head and said, "I run everything in my house. In the future all menus are to be approved by *me* and not by anybody else!"[13]

In December 1953 Press Secretary James Hagerty wrote the president a note indicating that NBC would be initiating the broadcast of color television in a few days and that the network was offering the loan of a color set to the White House. The president referred the memo to "Mrs. Eisenhower for decision" and her handwritten notation on the bottom of the memo reads, "Yes, I would like it in West Hall. [signed] MDE."[14]

She informed the White House staff of precise rules on everything from their use of the family elevator (forbidden) to forms of address (the chief usher was *Mr.* West, whereas servants were never to be addressed as "Mr." or "Mrs." but rather by first name). Mamie stopped the foot traffic between the east and west wings. "You are not to use the mansion as a passageway," she told both the president's staff and the social office.[15]

She also demanded perfection in all housekeeping chores. This reputation apparently traveled beyond the walls of the White House. In a 1957 letter from General Gruenther, now retired from NATO and the director of the American Red Cross, he thanked her for making the White House tour possible for 2,688 "Red Crossers." He went on to affectionately chide Mamie by noting that not only was the group thrilled at the opportunity to see the mansion, but "furthermore none found any dust in the corners in spite of the abbreviated cleaning period available to your staff."[16]

Mamie's rule over the Eisenhower household extended to budget matters

The Eisenhowers were perhaps the best-prepared host and hostess to enter the White House. Protocol was a way of life for them.

as well. "I always managed the money affairs of the family," she told Barbara Walters in a 1970 television interview.[17] The years of living on a company grade officer's income had ingrained a frugality in Mamie she never lost, even when Ike became president of the United States. From the security of the White House she commiserated with another "army wife," Mrs. Alfred Gruenther, upon the occasion of Gruenther's retirement from active duty, "At least in the Army we always knew what we were entitled to, also that Uncle Sam would take good care of us. The world outside is pretty cold and impersonal."[18]

As the "first lady" of Columbia University, her instructions to the president's household staff regarding the refrigerator included the admonitions: "no foods left in uncovered state — (wax papered, always)" and "Each day, contents looked over and all left-overs sent to kitchen."[19] Even in the White House, Mamie perused the daily newspapers for bargains in food, clothing, and household items. She often shopped by telephone, calling the store manager directly. "Go straight to the top. Don't fool around with some clerk," she advised the White House staff.[20] Her eagle-eye also made sure the billing for goods and services was always correct. In a letter to the first lady's social secretary, the Elizabeth Arden Salon was required to explain a believed discrepancy in their charges.

> Miss Holloway, hair stylist, has informed me that Mrs. Eisenhower told her on Saturday, May 11, 1957, that there is still some question in her mind regarding the credit for two bed jackets. . . . The bed jackets in question were returned to the New York Salon and subsequently transferred to Mrs. Eisenhower's Washington account and duly credited.[21]

Mamie's attention to financial details is revealed in another incident. Family friend and Colorado millionaire Aksel Nielson was overseeing the care of the old Doud family residence in Denver and wrote Mamie for permission to replace window awnings at $19.90 each. "I didn't feel I wanted to spend that money without your okay. If you will just mark the enclosed and mail it back to me, I will follow your instructions."[22]

First ladies are often used as a conduit by the general public to get their ideas or opinions to the man in the Oval Office. Mamie was no different, and her papers are filled with examples of this role. During the early months of 1952 when Ike was still commander of SHAPE, she received a letter from a devoted "Eisenhower for President" supporter with a suggestion for a campaign slogan to augment the popular "I like Ike" in the upcoming election. The proposed slogan, which played on the general's NATO role, was "Ike will put *us* in SHAPE." A military aide responded to the writer saying "Mrs. Eisenhower has asked me to thank you for your letter . . . she has put [it] aside for him to read in his first moment of leisure."[23]

Not just the general public, but the famous also approached Mamie as an avenue to Ike. World traveler and radio commentator Lowell Thomas wrote to Mrs. Eisenhower at Columbia University in 1948 suggesting they consider his area in beautiful Quaker Hill, New York, as a location for the permanent Eisenhower residence (the Eisenhowers eventually chose Gettysburg, Pennsylvania). Thomas wrote Mamie again in 1954 praising Ike's recent speech before

Fashionably dressed, Mamie Eisenhower joins dozens of young women at a reception for the finalists in the Betty Crocker Homemaker of Tomorrow contest in April 1960.

the Daughters of the American Revolution convention as a "tour de force" and taking the opportunity to ask the first lady if she would be interested in a demonstration of something new called "Cinerama." There is no record indicating a showing in the White House theater, but Lowell Thomas did succeed in getting invited to one of the president's "stag dinners" the following year."[24]

During the Eisenhower presidency, Mamie's relations with the press can perhaps best be characterized as cordial, but limited. She always carried out her role in public ceremonies in a cheerful and gracious manner but otherwise sought and received less publicity than several other recent first ladies. Shortly after entering the White House, Mamie turned down an offer by the New York *Herald Tribune* to write a daily piece entitled, "An Incident a Day in The Life of the First Lady." Publisher Bill Robinson strongly promoted the idea by emphasizing that the column would "reflect to the world the character and integrity which we now have at the head of our government" and "would have great effectiveness as a unifying force among Americans." Mamie declined, stating she could not become so definitely associated with a daily column. She went on to add that "It sounds like a terrible chore and smacks of [Eleanor Roosevelt's] "My Day" column, of which I have a perfect horror!"[25]

According to James Deakin, White House correspondent for the *St. Louis Post-Dispatch*, Jim Hagerty was the best presidential press secretary who ever lived. Deakin credits Hagerty with defining the role of the modern press secretary; his major duty being, in Hagerty's words, "to make the president look good."[26] Hagerty's "protective shield" over the president definitely extended to cover Mrs. Eisenhower as well. To prevent embarrassing situations, Hagerty had specific guidelines for the handling of White House press inquiries. At Mamie's request, he summarized them in a 1954 letter to her son, Maj. John Eisenhower, who was himself preparing to be interviewed by a newspaper writer doing a human interest story on the president's grandchildren. Hagerty wrote:

> As a precaution, I always talk to any writer first, just to make sure that he or she is all right—that they are not trying to slant their articles or that they have not been planted by someone we wouldn't like to have around. . . . We try to keep away from direct quotes and insist that neither the President nor Mrs. Eisenhower are quoted directly.[27]

This policy in practice is exemplified in a revealing memo from Hagerty advising the first lady's office to "stall" on a request by a female reporter for White House Social Office press credentials. Hagerty adds, "I would like to give you the fill-in on this orally and not in writing." After her conversation with Hagerty, Mary Jane McCaffree, the first lady's secretary, annotated the original memo with a handwritten note stating "Jim H says she is a 'bad' girl—Do not reply."[28]

In another example, an interview with Mamie by a *Look* magazine writer was declined. Murray Snyder, assistant White House press secretary, looked over the questions submitted prior to the planned interview by *Look* and observed that "they are excellent" and that they "provide the pattern for a fine magazine piece." The problem, he observed in a memo to Mary Jane McCaffree, was that "they embrace all the questions which the First Lady has studiously avoided answering for the past two years." Moreover, Murray noted that several of the major questions "impinge on the question of whether the President will run again in 1956."[29]

Mamie's popularity with the American public was due in large measure to her natural personality and sincere interest in other people. Her papers at the Eisenhower Library indicate, however, that her deserved positive image was protected whenever possible by the tireless efforts of the White House press office.

Soon after the November 1952 election, Mamie received a letter from Alice Hughes, whose column "A Woman's New York" appeared around the country as part of the King Features Syndicate. Ms. Hughes wrote,

> My dear Mrs. Eisenhower:
>
> It occurs to me you may have no notion how happy the women in the country are, that finally we shall have a woman in the White House who is fashion-aware. Both Mrs. Truman and Mrs. Roosevelt are fine human beings, but fashion was not forthcoming from them.[30]

Mamie did not disappoint America's fashion-conscious women. With her feminine dresses, matching hats, gloves, and shoes, and bangs styled by Elizabeth Arden Salons, she quickly established the "Mamie Look." Throughout the White House years, she was listed among the "ten best-dressed women" in the country. She even gave permission for the pink color used in her inaugural ball gown to be officially called "First Lady Pink."[31]

Mamie was undeterred by the early negative letters she received about her controversial hairstyle. In the "Appeal and Crank Letters" folder of the Columbia University Series, correspondence may be found from detractors who informed Mamie that "[you] would look nicer if you didn't wear your hair like a six year old kid" and that her bangs "only draw attention to an effort to cover up a high forehead."[32]

Not surprisingly, there was a practical side of Mamie's approach to fashion. The influence of her years as an army wife once again came through in a message she sent to editors attending the opening of 1953 Fashion Press Week.

> As a soldier's wife I learned early in life that pride in personal appearance is not a superficial thing. It rates high on every officer's efficiency report—and his family is part of that report. An army wife sometimes has fewer dresses than her husband has uniforms. Consequently my training has been to select carefully and wear my clothes a long time. Knowing what to look for and how to tell a lasting fashion from a temporary fad has always helped me to shop intelligently.[33]

Further evidence of Mamie's "practical philosophy" was seen in a response to Helen Thomas of United Press from the first lady's press secretary in September 1953. Thomas was informed that Mrs. Eisenhower was planning to wear "last season's clothes" and "will keep her hemlines at 13 inches" despite the fact that "Dior stirred up a hornet's nest by raising the hemlines."[34]

Mamie's influence on Eisenhower was truly fundamental. Before their marriage, Ike had lived in a fairly narrow environment in Abilene and at West Point. Mamie had been to finishing school, and her family was well traveled. Her affluent parents, in a sense, adopted Eisenhower and were important in his early development as a young man. Mamie's entering Eisenhower's life was a significant broadening influence. Kevin McCann, who assisted Ike with his books and speeches, went as far as saying, "Ike would have been *Colonel* Dwight D. Eisenhower, if it weren't for Mamie."[35]

In the White House, Mamie continued to exercise a substantial influence on Ike. He sought her advice on political personalities and respected her as a shrewd observer with an "uncanny and accurate judgement of people."[36] But as the president's appointments secretary, Tom Stephens, noted, Mamie belonged to a different era. She did not express political opinions or disagree with her husband the way politicians' wives do today.[37] Mamie Doud Eisenhower was not an activist first lady, but her papers at the Eisenhower Library provide great insight into the unique role she played. Granddaughter-in-law Julie Nixon Eisenhower recalled these words of wisdom from Mamie regarding life with "their Eisenhower men:" "There can be only one star in the heaven, Sugar, and there is only one way to live with an Eisenhower. Let him have his own way."[38]

Mamie maintained a secure refuge for her husband in the White House residence and strived to keep his hours of relaxation uninterrupted by the demands of the Oval Office. When asked in an interview one month before her death in November 1979 if today's presidents need their wives' help, she replied, "A man has to be encouraged. I think I told Ike every day how good I thought he was. Your ego has to be fed."[39]

NOTES

[1]Elizabeth Henney, "Presenting: Mrs. Eisenhower," *Washington Post*, Aug. 2, 1942, "Photographs, Newsclippings," White House Series, Mamie Doud Eisenhower Papers, Dwight D. Eisenhower Library, Abilene, KS.

[2]Marianne Means, *The Woman in the White House: The Lives, Times and Influence of Twelve Notable First Ladies* (1963), p. 237.

[3]J. B. West with Mary Lynn Kotz, *Upstairs at the White House: My Life with the First Ladies* (1973), p. 135.

[4]Katherine Howard to Mamie Doud Eisenhower, Oct. 8, 1953, "Howard, Mrs. Charles P. (Katherine)," White House Series, MDE Papers, DDE Library.

[5]Nina E. Warren to Mrs. Dwight D. Eisenhower, n.d., "War (1)," White House Series, MDE Papers, DDE Library.

[6]Mamie Doud Eisenhower to Mrs. Aksel Nielson, Apr. 29, 1953, "Nielson, Mr. and Mrs. Aksel," White House Series, MDE Papers, DDE Library.

[7]Means, *The Woman in the White House*, pp. 240–241.

[8]Mamie Doud Eisenhower to Gen. Alfred M. Gruenther, Nov. 17, 1952, "Gruenther (1)," White House Series, MDE Papers, DDE Library.

[9]Mrs. Richard Nixon to Mamie Doud Eisenhower, n.d. (c. Oct. 1955), "Nixon, Vice-President and Mrs. (Pat & Dick)," White House Series, MDE Papers, DDE Library.

[10]Stuart Symington to Mrs. Dwight D. Eisenhower, Feb. 20, 1953, "Su(2)," White House Series, MDE Papers, DDE Library.

[11]Nick Thimmesch, "Mamie Eisenhower at 80," *McCall's*, Oct. 1976, p. 212.

[12]Steve Neal, *The Eisenhowers: Reluctant Dynasty* (1978), p. 401.

[13]West, *Upstairs at the White House*, p. 131.

[14]Jim Hagerty to Dwight D. Eisenhower, Dec. 10, 1953, "T(2)," White House Series, MDE Papers, DDE Library.

[15]West, *Upstairs at the White House*, p. 133.

[16]Alfred M. Gruenther to Mamie Doud Eisenhower, n.d. (c. May–June 1957) "Gruenther (5)," White House Series, MDE Papers, DDE Library.

[17]Interview of Mamie Doud Eisenhower by Barbara Walters, Mar. 26, 1970, Augusta, GA, DDE Library audiovisual archives.

[18]Mamie Doud Eisenhower to Mrs. Alfred M. Gruenther, Apr. 24, 1956, "Gruenther (4)," White House Series, MDE Papers, DDE Library.

[19]C. Lent to Col. Robert L. Schultz, June 8, 1950, "Employees File (Current)," Columbia University Series, MDE Papers, DDE Library.

[20]West, *Upstairs at the White House*, p. 145.

[21]Mrs. Edna C. Pifer to Mrs. Mary Jane McCaffree, May 13, 1957, "Personal-MDE (2)," White House Series, MDE Papers, DDE Library.

[22]Aksel Nielson to Mrs. Dwight D. Eisenhower, June 3, 1960, "Nielson, Mr. and Mrs. Aksel," White House Series, MDE Papers, DDE Library.

[23]Dr. Daniel Barsky to Mrs. Dwight D. Eisenhower, Mar. 30, 1952, and Lt. Col. C. Craig Cannon to Dr. Daniel Barsky, Apr. 7, 1952, "B," SHAPE Series, MDE Papers, DDE Library.

[24]Lowell Thomas to Mrs. Dwight Eisenhower, June 7, 1948, Principal File Series, Dwight D. Eisenhower Pre-Presidential Papers, and Lowell Thomas to Mrs. Dwight Eisenhower, May 17, 1954, "Th(1)," White House Series, MDE Papers, DDE Library.

[25]William E. Robinson to Mrs. Dwight D. Eisenhower, Mar. 5, 1953, and Mamie Doud Eisenhower to William E. Robinson, Mar. 19, 1953, "Robinson, Mr. William (Bill)(1)," White House Series, MDE Papers, DDE Library.

[26]James Deakin, *Straight Stuff: The Reporters, the White House and the Truth* (1984), pp. 145, 156.

[27]James C. Hagerty to Maj. John Eisenhower, Mar. 29, 1954, "Press (1954)(1)," White House Series, MDE Papers, DDE Library.

[28]Jim Hagerty to Mary Jane McCaffree, Feb. 9, 1955, "Press Requests (2)," White House Series, MDE Papers, DDE Library.

[29]Murray Snyder to Mary Jane McCaffree, Jan. 31, 1955, "Press (1955–56)," White House Series, MDE Papers, DDE Library.

[30]Alice Hughes to Mrs. Dwight D. Eisenhower, Dec. 8, 1952, "Press Requests(2)," White House Series, MDE Papers, DDE Library.

[31]Mary Jane McCaffree to Mrs. Rorke of Textile Color Institute, Jan. 26, 1953, "T(2)," White House Series, MDE Papers, DDE Library.

[32]"A Friend" to Mrs. Ike, May 3, 1948, and "A Friend" to Mrs. Eisenhower, May 7, 1948, "Appeal and Crank Letters Written to Mrs. E(1)," Columbia University Series, MDE Papers, DDE Library.

[33]Message from Mrs. Eisenhower to Editors Attending Press Week, Jan. 5, 1952[*sic*], "Press Requests (1)," White House Series, MDE Papers, DDE Library.

[34]Helen Thomas to Mrs. Mary Jane McCaffree, Sept. 2, 1953, and Mary Jane McCaffree to Polly Canfield, n.d., "Press (1952–53)(2)," White House Series, MDE Papers, DDE Library.

[35]Thimmesch, "Mamie Eisenhower at 80," p. 212.

[36]Neal, *The Eisenhowers*, p. 401.

[37]Thimmesch, "Mamie Eisenhower at 80," p. 214.

[38]Julie Nixon Eisenhower, "Mamie," *Ladies Home Journal* (June 1977): 108.

[39]Interview of Mamie Doud Eisenhower by Barbara Walters, Oct. 1979, "20/20 News Magazine," DDE Library audiovisual archives.

An Enduring Fascination
The Papers of Jacqueline Kennedy

By *Mary Ann Watson*

Jacqueline Kennedy brought beauty, poise, and cultivated taste to the role of first lady.

"I hope that in the years to come many of you and your children will be able to visit the Kennedy Library," the widowed first lady said softly, haltingly on a network television broadcast on January 14, 1964. Deluged with over eight hundred thousand messages of sympathy and grief in the weeks after Dallas, Mrs. Kennedy chose to make a public statement on television to express her thanks to those who wrote to her of their love for the late president. Somehow, the mention of the plans for the library to be built in his memory made the ineffable sadness of the moment more bearable.

In retrospect, there was also a subtle irony in Mrs. Kennedy's remarks about the John F. Kennedy Library. "It will be, we hope, not only a memorial to President Kennedy," she said, "but a living center of study of the times in which he lived."[1] This immensely private young woman could not have known at the time that students and scholars of the New Frontier in years to come would examine her legacy as first lady with the same academic rigor devoted to world leaders and other key players of the era.

A portrait of American society during the Kennedy years is incomplete without a consideration of how Mrs. Kennedy so detachedly, almost begrudgingly, captured universal attention and affection. Her tenure as first lady came just before the blossoming of the women's movement that would revolutionize American life and also endow scholarly legitimacy on the historical evaluation of presidential partners. In the mid-1960s, as she worked diligently to make the Kennedy Library a reality, Mrs. Kennedy probably did not anticipate that it would someday become a center for the serious study of her life as well.

As the spouse of an American presidential candidate, Jacqueline Bouvier Kennedy was catapulted into the international limelight when she was just thirty-one years old. In late September of 1960, Mrs. Kennedy was a guest on the CBS program *Person-to-Person*. The host of the broadcast, Charles Collingwood, asked "What do you say should be the major role of the First Lady?" "Well," she replied, "I think the major role of the First Lady is to take care of the President so he can best serve the people. And not to fail her family, her husband, and children." "And what about the official duties?" Collingwood continued, "The social responsibilities?" "Well, of course, she can't expect to be a completely private person," the candidate's wife explained, "She will have an official role which she must play and accept with grace . . . I think there's so much she can do. Things she cares about she can help. In my case it would be education, helping children, student exchange and cultural programs abroad."[2] This agenda, of course, never came to pass.

As first lady, Mrs. Kennedy was not an activist. Perhaps because the mass media employed such little restraint in covering her family and herself, she felt she should not invite more media attention by championing causes. Perhaps she underestimated the magnitude of the tasks she described. Or perhaps it just seemed the right thing to say to Charles Collingwood at the time.

Mrs. Kennedy did not follow the pattern of a first lady taking on projects of social concern. She was often "unavailable" for events the first lady was traditionally expected to attend. As she once said when demurring from a series of public appearances, "After all, I'm *not* Mrs. Roosevelt."[3] Jacqueline Kennedy's reluctance to dutifully surrender her private life only magnified her mystique.

Time has not lessened the allure of Jacqueline Kennedy in our popular imagination. The fascination she holds for Americans is enduring. The historical collections at the Kennedy Library offer researchers the chance to extract and assimilate bits of information about Mrs. Kennedy that help us understand more clearly, though not completely, the woman and the era.

Traditional textual documents relating to the first lady are not abundant. Pierre Salinger's staff files are available, but they do not constitute a particularly rich vein to mine for clues to the personality of Jacqueline Kennedy. They include guest lists for White House functions and some logistical information about the activities. However, the slow process of opening Mrs. Kennedy's White House Social Files has begun. The first one hundred of fourteen hundred boxes have recently become available to researchers. Possibly, the information found in these files will add to what has already been written about the changes Mrs. Kennedy imposed on White House entertaining. The Social Files, which were the working files of the first lady's office, also include some fragmentary material about the White House restoration project. It is likely that the primary source documents preserved in the Social Files will add dimension to the enchanting photographs we have all seen of state dinners and world famous artists and literary figures at the White House—the pictures that to this day breathe life into the folk myth of Camelot.

The vast holdings of the research reference room at the Kennedy Library include hundreds of works pertinent to the study of Mrs. Kennedy's life. The array ranges from serious scholarship down to tawdry sensationalism. And that is its value. No attempt has been made to filter the acquisitions for dignity's sake. It is likely the copies of supermarket checkout-line magazines with screaming headlines tell us more about ourselves than Mrs. Kennedy, but they are all part of the climate of the era. They also help us understand her reserve. What so many have interpreted as coldness or aloofness might more accurately be read as self-protection.

Mrs. Kennedy's significant impact on fashion in the early 1960s is also preserved here for posterity. Helen Thomas of United Press International, one of the reporters who, by her own admission, "dogged Jackie," recalls in her autobiography, "We couldn't afford expensive wardrobes on a reporter's salary, though we conformed to Jackie's style with bouffant hairdos and the bare-arm look of the day, even though not all of us were built for it, I'll admit."[4] The

A pregnant Mrs. Kennedy poses with her husband and CBS host Charles Collingwood before her appearance on Person-to-Person *in 1960.*

inside story on the evolution of the first lady's "look" can be found in *I Was Jacqueline Kennedy's Dressmaker*, by Mini Rhea. We learn not only of her penchant for braided trim, but of her absolute certitude in what she wanted done. It is a character trait that surfaces in scores of accounts of Mrs. Kennedy's interactions with support staff of every kind . "When Jackie came to me to do her sewing," the dressmaker writes, "she was one of the few customers who didn't ask for a lot of advice. She accepted advice graciously—but usually ignored it. I was not insulted. I was happy about this because it meant that here was a woman who knew what she wanted—knew the look she was trying to achieve."[5]

The oral history collection at the Kennedy Library is another valuable source of illumination on the subject of Mrs. Kennedy. Between 1964 and 1974, approximately twelve hundred formal recollections of the Kennedy administration were gathered for the oral history project. Today, seven hundred transcripts are open to researchers. Though the president was the focus of the project, there is a great deal here concerning his wife. By carefully piecing together these fragmentary glimpses of Jacqueline Kennedy, one may begin to see beneath the public surface. Luminaries such as Leonard Bernstein and the late Princess Grace of Monaco related anecdotes of private moments with her. Mrs. Kennedy's irreverent sense of humor is admired in the reflections of statesmen who understood the art of socializing and appreciated her nontraditional approach.

Also in the oral history collection are the revealing remembrances of the men and women whose workaday lives revolved around Mrs. Kennedy's wishes. Those responsible for the electrical work, painting, upholstering, animal care, cleaning, and gardening at the Executive Mansion tell remarkably similar tales about the mistress of the house. Mrs. Kennedy had an extraordinary capacity for attention to detail. Things not done her way were things done over again. She was demanding, even difficult, but she was a woman who never took craftsmanship for granted. She appreciated work excellently done. The first lady was also a woman who never forgot a kindness. A painter recalled being asked to stay late one day to finish work on the children's rooms. A snowstorm forced him to spend the night at the White House. "She [Mrs. Kennedy] had supper sent up and breakfast the next morning," he said, "and the next morning she had the florist make up a beautiful cibidium [*sic*] orchid corsage, a double corsage, for my wife . . . She was very thoughtful—Mrs. Kennedy was."[6]

In their last mournful days of service to the Kennedy family, those on the White House staff once again marvelled at the first lady's command of arrangements. An usher at the mansion recalled that Mrs. Kennedy "radioed ahead from the plane to tell us exactly what she wanted. Of course, that afternoon was spent in finding the details—looking up the details of the Lincoln funeral so that we could have things as near as possible the way they were at the time Lincoln was assassinated."[7] A furniture craftsman with the restoration project was asked to help get the White House ready for the arrival of the president's body. "My wife and I worked with Mr. [Sargent] Shriver as to what had to be draped in black. My wife and I hung and draped black material until 4:30 in the morning just as Mrs. Kennedy accompanied the body to the White House."[8]

Though world leaders would soon be gathering in the capital and countless matters of protocol required attention, those whose labor eased the life of the president and his family were not overlooked. A White House maid recalled it was a hectic time,"but Mrs. Kennedy," she said, "had sent us all the little invitations to the funeral."[9]

Only now, almost a quarter of a century later, can we fully appreciate how appropriate it was for Mrs. Kennedy to use television in January of 1964 as the medium to reach the American public on her husband's behalf. After the 1960 presidential campaign, many believed that television had been responsible for John Kennedy's narrow margin of victory over Richard Nixon. It was Kennedy's masterful use of the medium that contributed in such large measure to the deep sense of personal loss so many citizens felt upon his death. And it was the ritual power of television that brought Americans through the tragedy with the faith that our democracy would maintain its course.

The Kennedy years coincided with a remarkable period of growth in the American television industry. Not only were great technological strides being made, but the networks were in the process of expanding news and public affairs programming as well. The 1960s was the decade in which television became truly central to American life.

The audiovisual records at the John F. Kennedy Library are a repository rich with the kinds of historical documents unique to the latter half of the twentieth century. Television programs, ostensibly ephemeral but now preserved on videotape, capture the temper of the times with compelling force. Through the tapes, a researcher can study how television became the most important way in which the American public came to know John and Jacqueline Kennedy. Because most of Mrs. Kennedy's public activity falls in the category of ceremonial functions, television documents her competent performance in abundant detail.

One of her first and happiest triumphs as first lady came in the spring of 1961. "I am the man who accompanied Jacqueline Kennedy to Paris and I have enjoyed it," the president quipped in response to the overwhelming reception she received in the French capital. Mrs. Kennedy's performance on this European tour was stunning and memorable for reasons beyond her wardrobe and hairstyles. She was much more than an ornament at the president's side. Mrs. Kennedy, because of her linguistic talents and genuine cultural erudition, was a partner in diplomacy.

On this trip Mrs. Kennedy amazed and delighted Charles de Gaulle with her grasp of French history. Acting as an interpreter for her husband and the French president, she created a relaxed atmosphere conducive to frank conversation. A warm respect developed between the men. "I now have more confidence in your country," de Gaulle said to President Kennedy upon his departure. The first lady also established a rapport with French cultural minister André Malraux. With his help she arranged the celebrated 1962 Washington exhibition of Leonardo's Mona Lisa.

A few weeks before the Kennedys visited Paris, a French television journalist interviewed Mrs. Kennedy at the White House. The videotape is available at the Kennedy Library.[10] Even a researcher unable to understand the French language can easily appreciate the impression the first lady made on the people of France as she playfully, almost flirtatiously, banters in French with the handsome questioner. There is an ease about her in this situation that rarely surfaced in American television interviews.

The American television networks covered every leg of President and Mrs. Kennedy's European tour on evening newscasts and with additional broadcasts such as the CBS News Special Report of June 4, 1961, "Gala in Vienna." The pageantry attendant to this summit meeting between the most powerful of world leaders is astonishing. "It could be described as dazzling," said correspondent Charles Kuralt, "but it would suffer from inadequacy."[11] When all was said and done, Nikita Khrushchev did not soften for the president. For Mrs. Kennedy he melted.

A state visit to South America in December of 1961 was referred to on a CBS News broadcast as "another Jackie Kennedy triumph."[12] A cut to President

Kennedy at the speaker's podium in Venezuela clarifies the reference. "Ladies and gentlemen," he said, "one of the Kennedys does not need an interpreter. So, I'd like to have my wife say a word or two." Her Spanish was not quite as fluent as her French, but Mrs. Kennedy's studied greetings nonetheless fell on delighted ears. To see the joyful audience reaction and hear the thunderous cheers gives one a palpable sense of international friendship.

On this trip, as on so many others, such as the Kennedys' visit to Mexico in the summer of 1962, it was reported that Mrs. Kennedy "stole the show." In the general biographical literature on President Kennedy there are numerous speculations that he resented the attention lavished upon his wife. The evidence of his true esteem for her, however, is not difficult to uncover. "You have no idea what a help Jackie is to me," he once told a family friend, "and what she has meant to me."[13] Despite purported marital strains, John Kennedy took pride in the accomplishments of his wife and never felt her successes diminished his stature.

A semiofficial trip to India and Pakistan in early 1962 by Mrs. Kennedy and her sister Lee Radziwill garnered effusive media coverage. At the Kennedy Library one can view seemingly endless footage of the first lady attentively watching exotic ceremonies and dances. It is not surprising that "fatigue" on the part of Mrs. Kennedy caused several activities to be cancelled. A USIA documentary on the trip, controversial because of its $45,000 production price tag, is also in the collection.

The television event for which Jacqueline Kennedy is most widely remembered is the 1962 CBS broadcast that documented her efforts with the White House Restoration Project.[14] The first lady's mission to make the White House a living symbol reflecting the presidency of the United States was undertaken with skillful determination. As the one-year project drew to a close, she was justifiably proud of what she had accomplished. She was convinced by Blair Clark, the vice president of CBS News, whose friendship with the president went back to their Harvard days, to participate in the television tour.

Public anticipation of the event was great. It was not the story of the president's house that compelled viewers, of course. It was the possibility that Jacqueline Kennedy would reveal something more about herself during the rare sixty minutes in which she willingly took her place on America's center stage.

"A Tour of the White House with Mrs. John F. Kennedy" aired on February 14, 1962, and three out of every four Americans in front of a television set were watching her. Even though the program was heralded as "an example of television at its best" in newspapers across the country, it was not Mrs. Kennedy's finest television appearance. Any observer with a modicum of objectivity could not deny that she seemed awkward and stilted. But in 1962 there was little objectivity in the mass media concerning Jacqueline Kennedy. Only Norman Mailer was brazen enough to be stinging in his criticism. In his *Esquire* magazine essay "An Evening With Jackie Kennedy," he wrote that Mrs. Kennedy walked

Mrs. Kennedy helps celebrate her daughter Caroline's fifth birthday. "If you bungle raising your children," she said, "I don't think whatever else you do matters very much."

through the tour "like a starlet who is utterly without talent." Mailer concluded that Jacqueline Kennedy was "a royal phony. . . . She was trying, I suppose, to be a proper First Lady and it was her mistake."[15]

Television programming used as historical artifact speaks volumes about Mrs. Kennedy in her official capacity as first lady. It does not, and cannot, satisfy our curiosity about Jacqueline Kennedy the person. She glows on the television screen, but it is a luster without texture. When videotape is studied in tandem with textual records, however, our portrait of Mrs. Kennedy—though still impressionistic—is a much richer one.

The audiovisual records at the Kennedy Library also contain several examples of the impact of the Kennedy family on popular entertainment. "The inclusion of a First Lady in satirical sketches is something relatively new for TV," wrote Jack Gould of *The New York Times* in his column on the spate of Kennedy gags appearing on prime time television programs in the fall of 1962. "Mrs. Kennedy with her many interests and travel, her distinctive speaking voice and individual coiffure is a celebrity in her own right," Gould continued.[16] He describes a sketch on the season opener of the highly rated "Jack Benny Show" involving a remarkable Jacqueline Kennedy lookalike. A videotape of the routine can be viewed at the Kennedy Library.[17] The inclusion of a Caroline "double" in the sketch, though innocuous, helps us understand the wisdom of Mrs. Kennedy's tenacity in protecting her children from such exploitation.

Jacqueline Kennedy's painful final triumph as first lady, of course, cannot be fully understood without a consideration of television. Although it seems impossible for those who lived through the New Frontier, there is now a generation of Americans well into adulthood born after the death of John Kennedy. However hackneyed it sounds, it is absolutely accurate to say that words cannot express the power of television imagery on the weekend of November 22, 1963. As one views Mrs. Kennedy in the most monumental of ceremonial functions, doing what must be done with breathtaking composure, it is clear that among her many gifts is what friends have described as "strength of character."

Perhaps, before the twentieth century draws to a close, one of the most intriguing women it has known will write her memoirs. Some have suggested it is her duty. This much, they say, she owes to history. But the historical collections of the John F. Kennedy Library offer strong testimony to the contrary. For whatever privileges Jacqueline Bouvier Kennedy Onassis was afforded while she was first lady of this country, the debt has long been paid.

Notes

[1]"Thank You Address by Mrs. Kennedy," Jan. 14, 1964, videotape #IPC: 6, Audiovisual Archives, John F. Kennedy Library, Boston, MA.

[2]Interview of Jacqueline Kennedy by Charles Collingwood, Sept. 29, 1960, "Person-to-Person," videotape #TNC: 152, Audiovisual Archives, JFK Library.

[3]Interview of August Heckscher, special consultant to President Kennedy on the arts, p. 51 of transcript, Oral Hist. Coll., JFK Library.

[4]Helen Thomas, *Dateline: White House* (1975), p. 16.

[5]Mini Rhea with Frances Spatz Leighton, *I Was Jacqueline Kennedy's Dressmaker* (1962), p. 308.

[6]Interview of Joseph Karitas, White House painter, p. 25 of transcript, Oral Hist. Coll., JFK Library.

[7]Interview of Nelson Pierce, White House usher, p. 8 of transcript, Oral Hist. Coll., JFK Library.

[8]Interview of Larry Arata, White House upholsterer, Oral Hist. Coll., JFK Library.

[9]Interview of Cordenia Thaxton, White House maid, p. 13 of transcript, Oral Hist. Coll., JFK Library.

[10]Interview of Jacqueline Kennedy by M. Cremosse, May 20, 1961, videotape #FON: 10C, Audiovisual Archives, JFK Library.

[11]Charles Kuralt, CBS News Special Report: "Gala in Vienna," June 4, 1961, videotape #TNC: 218, Audiovisual Archives, JFK Library.

[12]CBS News Special Report: "The President and Mrs. Kennedy in South America," Dec. 18, 1961, videotape #TNC: 220, Audiovisual Archives, JFK Library.

[13]Interview of Kay Halle by William M. McHugh, Feb. 7, 1967, p. 10 of transcript, Oral Hist. Coll., JFK Library.

[14]"A Tour of the White House with Mrs. John F. Kennedy," Feb. 14, 1962, videotape #TNC: 164, Audiovisual Archives, JFK Library.

[15]Norman Mailer, "An Evening With Jackie Kennedy," *Esquire* (July 1962): 57—61.

[16]Jack Gould, "TV: 3 Major Comics Gibe at Kennedy 'Dynasty,' " *New York Times*, Sept. 26, 1962.

[17]"Jack Benny Show," Sept. 25, 1962, videotape #TNC: 62, Audiovisual Archives, JFK Library.

A Journey of the Heart

The Papers of Lady Bird Johnson

By Nancy Kegan Smith

Perhaps no modern first lady has done more toward beautifying the nation's capital than Lady Bird Johnson.

The twentieth-century first lady, her influence on her husband and his policies, and her own handling of an office that traditionally has no legally prescribed functions, has recently become a topic of great interest. The press has focused a great deal of attention on Lady Bird Johnson's beautification efforts, Betty Ford's views on abortion and the ERA, Rosalynn Carter's inclusion in cabinet meetings, and Nancy Reagan's concern about drug abuse. Three former first ladies and two daughters have written books that give us rare personal insight into the trials and benefits of this unique position. The increasing attention devoted to first ladies has heightened the desire of scholars to know the nature and availability of materials on first ladies in the presidential libraries. In this article I hope to draw attention to the range of materials at the Lyndon Baines Johnson Library and illustrate how this material can be used to document the personal and official life of Mrs. Johnson as first lady.

Mrs. Johnson was a very busy first lady. Even during her years in the White House she continued to view her most important role as providing a relaxed family atmosphere for her husband and daughters. Although initially shy about making public presentations, she gave over 164 speeches. She founded and chaired the First Lady's Committee for a More Beautiful Nation's Capital, served as the honorary chairman of the Project Head Start program, was a member of the Committee for the Preservation of the White House, and acted as the president's representative on the committee responsible for the planning and building of the Johnson Library. She established and hosted the Women Doer Luncheons and presided over countless White House dinners, teas, luncheons, receptions, tours, and presentations. To highlight President Johnson's "See the U.S.A." program and while accompanying her husband on foreign visits, she traveled hundreds of thousands of miles. In quiet moments she took time to keep a diary recording historic occasions and to read and reply to much of her correspondence. In July of 1965 Bess Abell, Mrs. Johnson's social secretary, was already forced to write a memo to Presidential Special Assistant Marvin Watson requesting more office space in the Social Files office, the office responsible for handling the responsibilities of the first lady. Mrs. Abell gave as her justification that "Mrs. Johnson is involved in so many more projects than previous First Ladies, that she needs more room to store all the paper work that goes with them."[1]

Sharing a sincere and mutual enjoyment of one another's company, the first lady and a large crowd of black school children demonstrate what Southern hospitality is all about.

Two of the main files containing this abundance of material on Mrs. Johnson are a collection known as the White House Social Files, which contains over three thousand archives boxes documenting Mrs. Johnson's White House years, and her personal papers, which are on deposit at the library and will be given to the federal government sometime in the future. Mrs. Johnson's personal papers, though not currently available for research, include the following files: Taylor and Pattillo family correspondence, correspondence between Lyndon and Lady Bird, prepresidential files, diaries, speech cards, postpresidential papers, manuscripts and research materials for *A White House Diary*, Mrs. Johnson's notebooks, and personal files maintained by Dorothy Territo. When these files are made available, they will provide historians with a personal glimpse into the lives of President and Mrs. Johnson and will add further documentation of Mrs. Johnson's role as first lady.

Of the vast amount of material that is available in the Johnson Library, the White House Social Files are the largest of the library's files on Mrs. Johnson. These files were created during the White House years and contain material on the activities of Mrs. Johnson, her daughters, and the social activities of the president. In November 1983 the library instituted a policy that allows researchers to request materials for review from most of the major files that constitute the social files.

Researchers will find the wealth of this collection overwhelming. Included are materials concerning Mrs. Johnson's activities in her main areas of interest: conservation, education, children, and promotion of President's Johnson's "See the U.S.A." program. The files also show Mrs. Johnson's involvement in the 1964 Whistle Stop Campaign, Women Doer Luncheons, and the social obligations of the first lady, such as planning and hosting White House receptions, head-of-state dinners, entertainment, and the weddings of Luci and Lynda Johnson.

Mrs. Johnson's conservation activities are enumerated in the Beautification Files, which document the nationwide conservation programs and legislation spearheaded by Mrs. Johnson and the accomplishments of the Committee for a More Beautiful Capital, for which Mrs. Johnson served as chairman.[2] Researchers will find notes and transcripts of meetings of the committee, copies and drafts of Mrs. Johnson's beautification speeches, and documents charting the progress of each project sponsored by the committee in the District of Columbia. These files document the fight to get the Highway Beautification Act of 1965 passed, the conflicts over the Federal Aid to Highways Act of 1968, and the different opinions of the members of the committee as to the types of projects they should undertake in the District.

Besides the Beautification Files, there are four other main series within the White House Social Files: Social Files Alpha Files, Liz Carpenter's Subject Files, Bess Abell's Files, and the Social Entertainment Office Files. All of these files are available to researchers on a review-on-request basis.

The Social Files Alpha Files fill over two thousand archives boxes with correspondence between various individuals and groups and Mrs. Johnson or her office staff. This collection contains copies of all outgoing letters from her office and often the original incoming correspondence. This file is valuable for the scholar who is interested in tracing the relationship of a particular individual with Mrs. Johnson. A more personal side of Mrs. Johnson is revealed in her letters to relatives or close friends such as Mary Lasker and Jane Engelhard.

Elizabeth Carpenter served as Mrs. Johnson's press secretary and staff director. Her White House files are called the Liz Carpenter Subject Files and are one of the most important series of the Social Files. The eighty-eight archives boxes contain memorandums, correspondence, transcripts of meetings and Women Doer Luncheons, drafts and final copies of speeches, reports, and biographical and historical material on the Johnson family. These papers also provide background information on trips taken and speeches given by Mrs. Johnson and document many of the important public events involving Mrs. Johnson or her daughters.

Two other key files that are part of the White House Social Files and that contain a complete documentation of the varied social activities of the first lady are the files of Mrs. Johnson's social secretary, Bess Abell, and the Social Entertainment Office Files. Contained in these files are invitation lists, suggestions for possible guests at White House events, seating charts, correspondence regarding acceptances and regrets to these events, and detailed material on the arrangements for social functions.[3]

In addition to Mrs. Johnson's personal papers and the Social Office Files, there are other materials scattered throughout the library's collections dealing with her activities during the White House years. Numerous oral history transcripts are available that show a much more personal side of Mrs. Johnson. Of particular importance are the oral histories of Liz Carpenter, Sharon Francis, and Bess Abell. The Personal Papers of Nash Castro, who was head of the National Capital Region of the National Park Service, contain material on Mrs. Johnson's travels, the Committee for a More Beautiful Nation's Capital, the Committee for the Preservation of the White House, and personal correspondence between Castro and Mrs. Johnson.

Three main subject categories in the White House Central Files are concerned with Mrs. Johnson: FE 12/Johnson, L. B.; PP 5/Johnson, Lady Bird; and TR1/Johnson, Mrs. These files contain documentation on social and official appearances, her 1964 campaign trips and speeches, her involvement in the planning of the Johnson Library, and the issues that required the attention of both President and Mrs. Johnson or their staffs.

White House Famous Names is a special file that was created to maintain the president's correspondence with former presidents and others whose letters had historical significance or autograph value. In this file there are folders on Mrs. Roosevelt, Mrs. Truman, Mrs. Eisenhower, and Mrs. Kennedy. These files are of especially high quality and show a more personal side of the presidential families.

The importance of the excellent documentation available at the library on Mrs. Johnson can be shown by examining a few historical incidents and demonstrating how these files help in understanding the varied roles of a first lady and the range of issues handled by her office.

Two examples from the files illustrate Mrs. Johnson's role in advising and furthering President Johnson's civil rights program. At the Democratic National Convention in 1964, the Mississippi Freedom Democratic Party challenged the seating of the all-white regularly elected Mississippi Democratic delegation. They charged that this group had been picked in a way that excluded any black participation and therefore was not truly representative. Throughout August, civil rights leaders, including Martin Luther King, Jr., and Aaron Henry, contacted the president and asked him to publicly endorse the seating of the Mississippi Freedom Democratic delegates. Behind the scenes, President Johnson contemplated this thorny and controversial problem. In doubt as to the stand he should take, he asked Mrs. Johnson to draft a statement for him on this issue. The statement she drafted said:

> I believe the legal delegation ought to be seated. I am not going to bend to emotionalism. I don't want this convention to do so either. The election is not worth that.
>
> I am proud of the steady progress that has been made in the area of human and equal rights.
>
> In 1957, in 1960 and again in 1964, I was in the leadership to bring equal rights and decent progress to the Negro. I would not change a line of what has been passed or written. So long as I am President I will continue to lead the way within the guidelines of the law and within the framework of justice.[4]

Eventually a compromise was worked out by the Credentials Committee, and President Johnson did not use this draft. The document is important, however, because it shows that President Johnson so valued Mrs. Johnson's advice that he asked for her guidance on a potentially explosive key issue. It also helps us to understand Mrs. Johnson's own views—her strong defense of

In the White House, Lady Bird Johnson served as one of the president's top advisers and foremost advocates of administration policies. On the LBJ ranch outside of Austin, Texas, they enjoy a quiet walk together.

the civil rights program, but at the same time her desire to support what she felt was the legally elected group.

In October 1964 Mrs. Johnson set out on a campaign trip for President Johnson that became known as the Whistle Stop Campaign. This was the most public exposure Mrs. Johnson had in her political life, and at the outset, conditions did not promise a very favorable reception. She was going to ride a train from Alexandria, Virginia, to New Orleans, Louisiana, for four days stopping along the way in small towns and large cities to let the people of the South know that she and the president cared about them and felt they were an important part of the nation. Mrs. Johnson referred to it as "a journey of the heart."[5]

Although both President and Mrs. Johnson were from the South, the reception was expected to be hostile because they had strongly supported the Civil Rights Act of 1964, which had been passed in July. In Alexandria on October 6, 1964, Mrs. Johnson explained why she wanted to make this trip.

> I want to tell you from Alexandria to New Orleans that to this President and his wife the South is a respected and valued and beloved part of the country. I know that many of you do not agree with the Civil Rights Bill or the President's support of it, but I do know the South respects candor and courage and I believe he has shown both.
>
> It would be a bottomless tragedy for our country to be racially divided and here I want to say emphatically, this is not a challenge only in the South. It is a national challenge—in the big cities of the North as in the South.

The library's files on the Whistle Stop Campaign include drafts and final copies of the more than twenty-five speeches Mrs. Johnson made, plans for the trip, background on all the stops, and memorandums suggesting issues to be covered. One unsigned memo focused on the issue of education. "She would be a natural talking about education . . . TVA was FDR's dream for the South. Education can be the new dream and the ingredients are already at hand."[6] The Whistle Stop files document a unique political campaign, Mrs. Johnson's emergence as a public figure, the race question in 1964, and the importance of education in improving the quality of life in the South.

In 1965, to help with the balance-of-payments problem, President Johnson established a "See the U.S.A." program to encourage Americans to travel in their own country instead of abroad. Of the areas that Mrs. Johnson chose to focus on as first lady, this was the one that President Johnson had suggested and that was to remain a great concern throughout his presidency. He encouraged her to travel within the United States and to highlight its scenic spots. Since Mrs. Johnson had always loved nature, traveling to attract press attention to the "See the U.S.A." program was a natural choice. She often promoted both the president's program and the causes of beautification and education. The Liz Carpenter Subject Files contain complete records of these trips including planning memorandums, schedules, press releases and packets, and speeches. These trips show Mrs. Johnson capable of handling a variety of situations. She took reporters on a day-long raft trip down the Rio Grande; dedicated new dams, national parks, and seashores; visited with the poor in Appalachia; and delivered speeches at ivy league colleges. Here was an example of a happy partnership between a first lady and the press. She publicized her husband's policy of domestic travel and her concerns for beautification and education while reporters received new stories.

The far-reaching political implications of some of the social events handled by the first lady's office are illustrated by two incidents. In June 1965 President Johnson sponsored a White House Festival of the Arts to salute American artists and their supporters. The Social Files and other presidential files fully document the event and its complicated arrangements including scheduling invitations to artists and Mrs. Johnson's remarks. Although the festival was supposed to honor artists and be for their benefit, it turned into a political event. One of the invited guests was Robert Lowell, a prominent American poet, who was to read some of his poetry. Lowell initially accepted the invitation, but on May 30, 1965, he sent President Johnson a letter that he had also released to the *New York Times*.

> When I was telephoned last week and asked to read at the White House Festival of the Arts . . . I am afraid I accepted somewhat rapidly and greedily. . . . After a week's wondering, I have decided that I am conscience-bound to refuse. . . . Although I am very enthusiastic about most of your domestic legislation and intentions, I nevertheless can only follow our present foreign policy with the greatest dismay and distrust.[7]

This refusal, which was followed by others, overshadowed the original purpose of the festival. This incident demonstrates how Mrs. Johnson's Social Files not only document the social arrangements and scheduling for a White House event, but also tell the story of a very controversial political occasion. In this case, these files illustrate President and Mrs. Johnson's support and encouragement for the arts and an early criticism of his administration's Vietnam policies.

A second example of a social occasion taking on political implications is drawn from one of the Women Doer Luncheons. To highlight the achievements of women during the 1960s, Mrs. Johnson held sixteen luncheons from 1964 to 1968, with a guest speaker or speakers at each one. The topics included the space program, city planning, beautification, training for underprivileged women, and crime. The library has invitations, regrets, guest lists, correspondence, and transcripts for these luncheons. Most were pleasant occasions that achieved their purpose of focusing on important issues that women were addressing. However, the luncheon on January 18, 1968, which was considering the subject of crime in the streets, ended up, to quote Mrs. Johnson, "explosively." Eartha Kitt, a well-known actress and singer, had been invited to this luncheon because of her activities with underprivileged youth. In the question and answer period that followed the presentations, she decided to make a speech. The basic thrust of Ms. Kitt's comments was that much of the problem of juvenile delinquency in America was attributable to young people being angry over the Vietnam war. "They are angry because the parents are angry. . . . The parents are angry because we are so highly taxed and because there is a war going on that the Americans do not understand." She went on to say, "This nation depends on strength; it depends on men who are strong. You take the best of the country and send them off to a war and they get shot. They [young people] don't want that." After Ms. Kitt finished her comments, Mrs. Hughes, the wife of the governor of New Jersey, rose to speak in favor of the policies of the Johnson administration. Mrs. Hughes, the mother of eight sons, declared that her children would serve if they had to, and she did not feel the Vietnam war was just any justification for juvenile delinquency. Mrs. Johnson also commented saying, "Because there is a war on, and I pray that there will come a just and honest peace, that still does not give us a free ticket not to try to work on bettering the things in this country that we can better."[8]

After this luncheon, Mrs. Johnson received a large amount of mail both supporting and condemning Eartha Kitt's comments. All of these letters, plus a complete record of what happened at the luncheon, are available in the White House Social Files. Once again these files show that such nationally significant topics as crime and the Vietnam war not only concerned President Johnson and his staff, but also very much affected the first lady's staff in the East Wing of the White House.

Mrs. Johnson's active participation in the Committee for the Preservation of the White House and the planning of the Johnson Library demonstrate her involvement in a wide variety of issues. When Mrs. Kennedy was first lady, she decided that the White House needed a total restoration. Mrs. Johnson felt a strong sense of responsibility to continue the excellent work started by Mrs. Kennedy and her Fine Arts Committee. In 1964 an executive order established the Committee for the Preservation of the White House. The order stated the belief "that the White House is not simply the home of the President. Its rooms, its furniture, its countless mementos made it a living story of the whole experience of the American people."[9] All of the meetings of this group were held at the White House under the direction of Mrs. Johnson. In Liz Carpenter's

A tireless first lady, Mrs. Johnson delivered more than 160 speeches, founded the First Lady's Committee for a More Beautiful Nation's Capital, and served on numerous other committees including the planning board for the LBJ presidential library.

Subject Files folder for this committee there are transcripts of meetings, lists of members and donations, and memorandums preparing Mrs. Johnson for upcoming meetings or informing her of potential acquisitions.[10]

Mrs. Johnson stressed the collection of Americana, and her personal taste is revealed throughout Liz Carpenter's files. Of a recently acquired bronze by Charles Russell called "Meat for Wild Men," she commented that it is "full of danger and earthiness and lusty strength, of the old west . . . I like to have this great big continent represented art-wise here."[11] For the new White House china she chose a wildflower pattern representing flowers from the fifty states and insisted that it be made in the United States. These files are important because they reveal a more personal side of Mrs. Johnson and show the artistic and cultural taste of many of the best art experts in this country. The Committee for the Preservation of the White House still survives, and by studying the files of several presidential administrations, scholars can document not only changing trends in the arts, but also one of the few official responsibilities of a modern first lady.

By August 1965 President Johnson had received a proposal from the University of Texas at Austin to build his presidential library. Mrs. Johnson wrote President Johnson the following note: "Sometime today if possible read the paper on your desk—proposal of the U. of Texas to GSA & Archives re LBJ Library & tell me what you think of it. Your loving wife."[12] At this early junction in the planning for the Johnson Library, Mrs. Johnson was already one of the president's chief advisers. Once President Johnson accepted this proposal and a later one establishing an Institute of Public Affairs, he relied on Mrs. Johnson to be his eyes and ears on this important project. The library's files on this subject in FE 12/Johnson, Lyndon B. and Social Files Alpha File for "Presidential Library" document Mrs. Johnson's comments on memorandums concerning the overall concepts for the library and school, undertaking the solicitation of papers, and attending library planning and museum exhibit meetings.

Personal glimpses of Mrs. Johnson are revealed in the transcripts for the library meetings. On March 28, 1968, when former Presidential Special Assistant Horace Busby suggested that the library needed an exhibit to explain the relationship between the Johnsons and the University of Texas, Mrs. Johnson countered, "It seems to me it is answering a question that hasn't been asked. . . . This is home. This is where we live, this is where we left a mark, if any." In a later meeting on exhibits, Mrs. Johnson suggested leaving space for "an exhibit on the relationship of the politician to the people, because that to me, is one of the richest, greatest stories, I love it."[13] Both files record Mrs. Johnson's advice on a variety of complex legal, historical, technical, and aesthetic questions, while at the same time revealing to scholars a more intimate side of her personality.

In addition to the files I have mentioned, there are other resources available to scholars interested in studying Mrs. Johnson and other first ladies. The Johnson Library can provide a list of oral histories and a list of the files on Mrs. Johnson. The White House Office of the Curator has materials available on both the Fine Arts Committee and the Committee for the Preservation of the White House. The Library of Congress has many of the papers of nineteenth- and early twentieth-century first ladies and their associates. All of these sources are valuable to students of this misunderstood office.

Mrs. Johnson referred to her Whistle Stop Campaign as a "journey of the heart." From looking at a sampling of her activities as first lady, I find this phrase applicable not only to her one campaign tour, but also to her White House years in general. She focused her attention on things she loved and knew and brought her special touch to the job of first lady in many ways. The papers of Mrs. Johnson at the Johnson Library, a few of which are highlighted in this essay, hold great wealth for historians who want to research and comment on her journey.

Notes

[1]Bess Abell to Marvin Watson, memo, July 13, 1965, EX PP 5/Johnson, Lady Bird, Mrs., box 62, White House Central Files (WHCF), Lyndon Baines Johnson Library, Austin, TX.

[2]Lewis L. Gould has used the Beautification Files as a source for several articles and a forthcoming book, *Lady Bird Johnson and the Environment: A First Lady's Commitment.* Some of Gould's articles dealing with first ladies and Mrs. Johnson include "First Lady as Catalyst: Lady Bird Johnson and Highway Beautification in the 1960s" *Environmental Review* 10 (Summer 1987): 77–92; "First Ladies" *The American Scholar* 55(Autumn

1986): 528–535; and "Lady Bird Johnson and Beautification," in Robert A. Divine, ed., *The Johnson Years, Volume Two* (1987).

[3]Bess Abell's Files and the Social Entertainment Office Files were used extensively by Elise Kirk in researching *Music at the White House* (1986).

[4]Draft statement by Mrs. Johnson, Aug. 31, 1964, EX PP 5/Johnson, Lady Bird, Mrs., box 62, WHCF, LBJ Library.

[5]Press release copy of Mrs. Johnson's speech in Alexandria, VA, Oct. 6, 1964, p. 3, LBJ Library.

[6]"Whistle Stop 10/13–16/64," memo, n.d., p. 1, box 11, Liz Carpenter's Subject Files, White House Social Files (WHSF), LBJ Library.

[7]Robert Lowell to President Johnson, May 30, 1965, "White House Festival of the Arts 6/14/65 folder 3 of 4," box 11, Bess Abell's Files, WHSF, LBJ Library.

[8]"Women Doers Luncheon—1/18/68," transcript of the Jan. 18, 1968, luncheon, box 45, Liz Carpenter's Subject Files, WHSF, LBJ Library.

[9]Report of the Committee for Preservation of the White House, box 5, Personal Papers of Nash Castro, LBJ Library.

[10]"White House Preservation Committee," box 66, Liz Carpenter's Subject Files, WHSF, LBJ Library.

[11]Transcript of meeting, Nov. 18, 1967, p. 13, "White House Preservation Committee," box 66, Liz Carpenter's Subject Files, WHSF, LBJ Library.

[12]Mrs. Johnson to President Johnson, c. May 30, 1966, EX FE 12/Johnson, L. B./1, box 15, WHCF, LBJ Library.

[13]Transcripts of meetings, Mar. 28, 1968, p. 4 and Jan. 8, 1969, p. 84, EX FE 12/Johnson, L. B./2-1/Audio Visual, box 16, WHCF, LBJ Library.

"She Deserved So Much More"
The Papers of Pat Nixon

By *Paul A. Schmidt*

Patricia "Pat" Ryan Nixon is a self-made woman who has overcome many personal hardships. She met the troubled days of "Watergate" with dignity and strength.

Richard Nixon once claimed that "any lady who is First Lady likes being First Lady. I don't care what they say. They like it."[1] Despite this assertion, Pat Nixon merely endured being first lady, even though it certainly had many pleasurable and memorable moments. She admirably performed the duties expected of her and went out of her way to bring the White House and the presidency to the people, but it would be a misstatement to say that she saw being the first lady as an enviable position. It was a privilege she would have preferred to have foregone.

About six months before President Nixon's resignation from office, J. Bernard West, former chief usher at the White House (he retired shortly after the Nixon's came to the White House in 1969), reminisced about his twenty-eight years of service and attempted to characterize the six previous first ladies. Concerning Mrs. Nixon, he astutely observed, "As for having to live in the White House, it was my distinct impression that Mrs. Nixon was unhappy about that. She seemed *most* reluctant."[2] President Nixon, in a 1982 interview, was somewhat more insightful regarding his wife's feelings: "Even though Pat doesn't really care for social life, . . . she is an excellent hostess who does it all very well. She's very good *onstage*, so to speak, even though she prefers not to be onstage."[3]

All of Pat Nixon's reluctance did not preclude her from becoming one of the most beloved of recent first ladies. She probably did more for her husband's presidential career than any previous first lady (save, perhaps, Eleanor Roosevelt). She traveled more than any other politician's wife before her and said of her relationship with the president, "We've always been a team."[4] In his memoirs, Richard Nixon said of his wife "she held to her guiding principle: the right of a woman to choose her role in life. And by her actions she proved that it was possible to be both an independent woman and a supportive wife."[5]

Pat Nixon's role in life was to be the wife of Richard Nixon, to campaign for him, to serve as his hostess, and to spread a warmth that contrasted with her husband's awkward formality. Mrs. Nixon's public reticence was often perceived as a shyness or, more harshly, as plasticity. It was more often a relapse into private reflection, an effort at retaining at least some of the privacy that she had forfeited to her husband's ambition.

Pat Nixon was uniquely suited to being first lady. Her experience as the

Pat Nixon enjoys the company of National Easter Seals child, Joann Schaffer. A woman of compassion, Mrs. Nixon used her influence as first lady to encourage volunteer service—"the spirit of people helping people."

wife of a congressman, senator, and vice president had given her an extensive familiarity with world leaders and customs. She knew well the Washington social scene and was used to entertaining on a grand scale. Patti Matson, a member of Mrs. Nixon's staff, once told Julie Eisenhower, "Your mother was always a professional. She took being First Lady seriously in the sense that she understood the pedestal the American people place their First Ladies on. I never got the impression that she put herself on the pedestal in personal terms, but rather that she knew what being First Lady meant to others."[6]

She took up her duties with relative ease and concentrated on what could be done on an individual basis for the betterment of America. She refused to adopt a "project" that would be her single signature of the Nixon presidency. Instead, she tried to reach out in various fields, in different ways. One of her main efforts was in extolling the concept of volunteerism among Americans. She said that, "by working where they are needed, alone or in groups, I feel that individuals can often accomplish things that legislation alone cannot. This is where I think I can help, encouraging what my husband has called those 'small, splendid efforts' of people trying to make life better for others. I believe there is an unusual quality about the American people—we have a long history of helping others."[7] Her first public appearance tour as first lady was a promotion of volunteerism on the West Coast. President Nixon noted, however, that "she bridled at the idea that volunteerism was her 'project,' or that her interests had to be compartmentalized."[8]

Mrs. Nixon took great pride in the White House and its history. The house was in great need of refurbishing by the time the Nixons moved in, and Pat was instrumental in refurnishing and redecorating fourteen rooms, most of them in the public section of the mansion. She so painstakingly sought out antiques and raised money for this project that by the time the Nixons left the White House there were twice as many historic pieces as when they had moved in five and a half years earlier. White House curator Clement Conger noted that Mrs. Nixon transformed "what he characterized as the 'average' White House collection into the 'preeminent collection in the country.' "[9] In addition to focusing on the interior of the house, Mrs. Nixon also had the exterior of the building illuminated.

As the wife of the president, Pat Nixon embarked on goodwill missions to various parts of the world. She was the first first lady to travel abroad as the president's official representative when she visited Peru, bringing donated American supplies to the victims of a recent powerful earthquake. This act of selflessness earned her the Grand Cross of the Order of the Sun from the president and people of Peru, an award she cherished greatly. Her trips to South America and to Africa further endeared her to the peoples of those continents. Her activities during the presidential trips to the Soviet Union and to the People's Republic of China went far toward establishing closer ties with those nations.

Despite some opposition to the women's liberation movement in general, Mrs. Nixon was a proponent of women's rights. She felt that female candidates for elective office were wholly acceptable and even tried to induce the president to select a woman for the Supreme Court.

Coral Schmid, a member of the first lady's staff, wrote to Mrs. Nixon declaring that, "you care about people. You do not need a special project or a catchy slogan. . . . Through interests and activity and a pet project one can endeavor to beautify the environment, upgrade education and improve the standard of living. But a special project does not heal the broken heart, eliminate hatred, loneliness and suffering—*it takes love*. And you care about our most precious resource—people. This is the gift you have given to our country."[10]

One of Mrs. Nixon's more pronounced public character traits was her steadfast loyalty to the president and her stamina and control in the face of the Watergate revelations. She was unwavering in support of her husband's innocence and, though she suffered internally with each new attack, she put on a brave face for her family and the nation. Julie Nixon Eisenhower recalled that "Although I did not see it at the time, Mother was indeed the one holding it all together. In the pre-Watergate years she seemed fragile. We had worried about her and wanted to protect her. Now she was the strongest of all."[11]

The final months took quite a toll on Pat Nixon, however. Despite the release of much of the tension, which was brought about by President Nixon's resignation in August 1974, she did not fully recover her former strength of purpose. From a woman who claimed in a 1971 interview that "I'm never tired," "I am never afraid," and "I don't get ill,"[12] she emerged as older, largely alone, and subject to bouts of debilitating illness. Richard Nixon, recalling his last day as president, summed up his wife's legacy and her fortitude at the end of a difficult time. "I knew how much courage she had needed to carry her through the days and nights of preparations for this abrupt departure. Now she would not receive any of the praise she deserved. There would be no round of farewell parties by congressional wives, no testimonials, no tributes. She had been a dignified, compassionate first lady. She had given so much to the nation and so much to the world. Now she would have to share my exile. She deserved so much more."[13]

The function of the East Wing, or first lady's office, is much the same as the president's operation in the West Wing, though on a smaller scale. Until recent years there has been little expected from the president's wife aside from presiding at formal social events. While this still occupies much of the first lady's time, she also has become engaged in humanitarian and other pressing social issues of the time. She has largely become a personality in her own right. To achieve these goals, the first lady's office has greatly increased in size and importance. Mrs. Nixon's staff assisted her in scheduling her activities, answering her correspondence, dealing with the press in public relations efforts, and planning social functions at the White House. This they often did without assistance, and sometimes with opposition, from the West Wing. The president's assistants often neglected to inform the first lady's staff of proposed events, thereby leaving them without guidance or completely out of the picture. This kind of antagonistic attitude caused a rift between the offices that simmered for years. "Pat Nixon's staff believed that the opposition to the First Lady was compounded of one part ignorance of her true value, one part jealousy, and one part male chauvinism."[14]

Though somewhat hampered by the West Wing, Mrs. Nixon's staff attempted to carry on their duties as best they could. The first lady's office records are known as the Social Files and are part of the White House Central Files. They are filed separately with a filing scheme and arrangement that parallels the Central Files. In addition to containing records generated by and about Mrs. Nixon, the Social Files also include material relating to the official schedules and duties of the Nixon daughters and their husbands.

The Nixon Social Files comprise almost seven hundred cubic feet of material. At this time none of the material is open for research. The main reason for the present inaccessibility of the records stems from a court order enjoining the National Archives to first process and open Watergate-related materials. Now that the targeted Special Files have been released to the public, archivists are able to turn to other files. Processing has just begun on the First Lady's Appointments Office, which comprises about twenty-five cubic feet of material.

Within the Social Files are subject categories and name files as well as the working records of Mrs. Nixon's staff. The staff was divided into five offices, namely Administrative, Appointments/Scheduling, Press Relations, Correspondence, and Social Secretary. The Administrative Office, headed by Constance Stuart from October 1969 to March 1973, was in charge of the overall East Wing staff as well as the domestic staff of the White House. Pat Nixon retained ultimate control over her staff but delegated many of the responsibilities to others.

The Appointments/Scheduling Office dealt with invitations sent to the first family and kept a careful catalog of schedules for Mrs. Nixon, Julie and David Eisenhower, and Tricia and Edward Cox. Also among the materials of the office are Mrs. Nixon's copies of briefing books for head-of-state visits to the White House and for foreign visits she and the president undertook. There are numerous photo albums in the collection on subjects relating to travel, the president's home at San Clemente, the second inauguration, and miscellaneous events at the White House. The Appointments Office records are contained in the files of Susan Porter, who had charge of the office during the second term. Also included in this collection are the first-term files of Coral Schmid and Stephanie Wilson.

The first lady's Press Office was concerned with issuing press releases for first family activities and dealing with the press in general. The files contain photos and clippings as well as correspondence on public relations matters. The Press Office records are contained in the files of Helen Smith, Mrs. Nixon's press secretary.

Aboard Air Force One. Mrs. Nixon often spent four hours a day reading and answering her mail. She also traveled extensively both with the president and as his "Personal Representative."

The Correspondence Office dealt with sending letters, cards, recipes, etc. in response to mail received by the first family. The incoming correspondence was generally filed in the Social Files name file. Mrs. Nixon spent a great deal of time reading and answering her mail—so much so that some thought that her time could be put to better use. Julie Eisenhower noted that "Every week, an average of one to two thousands letters arrived for Pat Nixon (the number always rose to around four thousand after an appearance on television or a foreign trip), and, without fail, my mother read nearly every letter and tried to see that everyone received a response. Many times she spent four or five hours a day on mail, usually working in the evening after dinner. No First Lady had received this volume of weekly mail before."[15] The Correspondence Office files are contained in the records of Gwendolyn King, the head of that office.

Social aspects of the White House were handled by Lucy Winchester, the social secretary. Her files include details surrounding White House church services (a Nixon innovation), "Evenings at the White House," state dinners, and other formal events in which Mrs. Nixon would have had a part. This office had close contact with the Social Entertainment Office under Sanford Fox, whose records would be tangential to East Wing operations.

The Central Files subject category PP, which contains first family material of a personal or quasi-personal nature, also will be of interest to researchers of the first lady's office. These records have not yet been processed.

Unlike the textual material of the first lady's office, most of the audiovisual record of Mrs. Nixon's activities is open for research. The White House Photo Office collection comprises approximately 370,000 images. Copies of photographic contact sheets featuring the first family have been segregated and total about 87,500 images. In addition, the extensive Naval Photographic Center White House Film Unit collection documents the first lady's activities, and copies of "shot cards" for films depicting Mrs. Nixon have been segregated in the first lady's Press Office files. The General Motion Picture Film File also has film footage of the first lady, but this collection has not been processed.

The White House Communications Agency (WHCA) files contain 172 audiotapes featuring remarks and speeches by Mrs. Nixon and 15 tapes with Connie Stuart. Also in that collection are 8 videotapes that contain footage of Mrs. Nixon, and 3 of Mrs. Stuart.

Staff members of the National Archives conducted exit interviews of departing White House staff during and after the Nixon administration as the beginning of an oral history program. Many of these interviews have been transcribed. Members of the first lady's staff who were interviewed were Penelope Adams, Mrs. Nixon's television and radio coordinator; Coral Schmid; and Constance Stuart. Interviews with William Codus, who was in charge of first family scheduling during the 1972 campaign, and Sanford Fox would also contain information relating to the operation of the office. These interviews are not open to the public at this time, but processing has begun on the collection. An oral history program has recently been initiated by the Nixon Materials staff, and interviews with former members of the first lady's staff will be scheduled.

Though not research material per se, the Nixon Gift Collection contains numerous head-of-state gifts and gifts presented to the first lady by American citizens. Some of the head-of-state gifts can be made available for public in-

In August 1970, Mrs. Nixon decided to build the confidence of inner-city children at D.C. Recreation Camp by showing them that hammering a nail was even more difficult than they had found it to be.

spection by appointment. The other gifts are not yet available to the general public.

Since the textual record of Pat Nixon's years in the White House is still closed, little can be added to the picture of her daily activity as first lady. In the years to come, as files are opened to the public, a new composite may be drawn of her and a new dimension may emerge. Until that time, we must be satisfied with what has already been reported in the press and through reminiscenses by family and friends. A complete and objective view of Pat Nixon is still to come.

NOTES

[1]Quoted in Lester David, *The Lonely Lady of San Clemente* (1978), p. 128.

[2]Peer J. Oppenheimer, "Our First Ladies, as We Never Knew Them, By a Man Who Served Them All," *Family Weekly* (Jan. 20, 1974): 5.

[3]Aileen (Suzy) Mehle, "Richard Nixon: 'My Wife Pat,' " *Good Housekeeping* (Aug. 1982): 156.

[4]Interview of Pat Nixon by Virginia Sherwood, Sept. 12, 1971, "A Visit with the First Lady," ABC Television.

[5]Richard M. Nixon, *RN: The Memoirs of Richard Nixon* (1978), p. 537.

[6]Julie Nixon Eisenhower, *Pat Nixon: The Untold Story* (1986), p. 416.

[7]"First Lady on Community Service: 'Caring for Others Creates the Spirit of a Nation,' " *U.S. News and World Report* (Aug. 2, 1971): 54.

[8]Nixon, *RN*, p. 536.

[9]Eisenhower, *Pat Nixon*, p. 263.

[10]Ibid., p. 364.

[11]Ibid., p. 417.

[12]Jessamyn West, "The Real Pat Nixon: An Intimate View," *Good Housekeeping* (Feb. 1971): 124, 127.

[13]Nixon, *RN*, p. 1086.

[14]David, *Lonely Lady*, p. 165.

[15]Eisenhower, *Pat Nixon*, p. 322.

"If There Was Anything You Forgot to Ask. . . ."
The Papers of Betty Ford

By Karen M. Rohrer

The leading feminist among modern first ladies, Betty Ford celebrates her husband's proclamation of international women's year.

Like her husband, Betty Ford did not seek the duties she assumed on August 9, 1974. In fact, she was reluctant to become first lady, even somewhat defensive. "I figured, okay, I'll move to the White House, do the best I can, and if they don't like it, they can kick me out, but they can't make me be somebody I'm not."[1] That was how she described her feelings when unique circumstances, beginning with the resignation of Spiro Agnew as vice president and culminating with the resignation of Richard Nixon as president, propelled her husband from minority leader of the House of Representatives to president of the United States. By the time she left the White House two and a half years later, there was a certain vocal faction of the American public who felt that she *should* be kicked out. However, the majority of people, according to the polls, felt that she had brought a breath of fresh air, and a great deal of courage, to the "office" of first lady.

Becoming first lady brings with it a great potential for influence. Some first ladies have chosen to remain in the background, performing only the expected ceremonial duties. Others have used the position as a platform from which they could promote projects and causes of special interest to them. Even those who have sought to use the power at their disposal have generally restricted themselves to noncontroversial topics that would not cause political repercussions for their husbands. Mrs. Ford believed that the country was ready for a first lady with a mind of her own and the courage to speak it.

Having lived in Washington political circles for twenty-five years, Mrs. Ford knew the magnitude of the "job" of being first lady. Although she had been in the spotlight before, as a professional dancer and model as well as a fashion coordinator for a department store, she confessed to being frightened of the prospect. Responsibility was nothing new to Mrs. Ford, however. The more powerful Gerald Ford had become in Congress, the more Betty Ford had had to shoulder the burden of raising four children. She has written that in 1965 "the House got a new Minority Leader and I lost a husband."[2] Her husband was out of town as many as 258 days of the year and the stress took its toll both physically and mentally. After that rough time in her life, Mrs. Ford sought therapy with a psychiatrist who helped her regain a feeling of self-worth and importance. By 1974 her children were grown, or nearly so, and she was ready to resume a career—ready to accomplish something on her own. Of her early

Betty Ford's liberal views on abortion, marijuana use, and premarital sex were candidly discussed with Morley Safer on CBS's "60 Minutes." Responses to her controversial remarks were both adamantly critical and supportive.

days in the White House, Mrs. Ford has written, "In the beginning, it was like going to a party you're terrified of, and finding out to your amazement that you're having a good time."[3]

By 1974 the demands on the first lady had become so complex that a support staff of about twenty-eight people had developed in the east wing of the White House. Mrs. Ford had a press secretary, personal assistants, a correspondence secretary, and an entertainments secretary, as well as their staffs. The files these offices maintained, now part of the holdings of the Gerald R. Ford Library, document the highs and lows, as well as the sheer work, of being first lady. The files, when they arrived at the library, totaled more than four hundred cubic feet—approximately one million pages. Sampling and disposal of some of the more mundane materials, such as greeting cards and general public correspondence, has lowered the figure slightly. Of the remaining materials, the most significant collections have been processed and made available for research. These include the files of Sheila Weidenfeld, Mrs. Ford's press secretary; Frances Kaye Pullen, speechwriter for the first lady; Elizabeth M. O'Neill, director of correspondence; and the trip files, local events case files, and magazines series of the Betty Ford Papers. In addition, general public mail samples on specific subjects can be made available to researchers who request them in advance.

Researchers will also find material relating to Mrs. Ford in the files of Patricia Lindh and Jeanne Holm, special assistants for women's programs in the Public Liaison Office of the President's Staff. The White House Central Files contain a wealth of material. The Subject File is an alphanumeric system of sixty primary subject categories, such as "PP" (President-Personal) and "SP" (Speeches), and over one thousand subcategories. The subcategory "PP5-1" (Ford, Betty) contains approximately three thousand pages documenting Mrs. Ford's activities. Cross-references to material filed under other Central Files codes are included. Perusal of the various files reveals the many ways in which Mrs. Ford reacted to and used the power of her position as first lady.

At her first press conference, Mrs. Ford announced that she intended to concentrate on promoting the arts and programs for underprivileged and retarded children, as well as on working for the passage of the Equal Rights Amendment. She had not even had time to organize her own staff or sort out her duties, however, when an unexpected discovery brought home to her the full extent of the first lady's ability to reach and affect the people of the country.

On September 28, 1974, less than two months after her husband's swearing-in as president, Mrs. Ford learned she had breast cancer. She allowed her illness and subsequent mastectomy to be discussed openly with the press in a conscious effort to reap a benefit from the tragedy. Mrs. Ford was an inspiration to other women who had been dealt the same blow, and the publicity has been credited with saving the lives of many women who would not otherwise have discovered tumors early enough to treat. A prime example was Happy Rockefeller, the vice president's wife, who underwent a double mastectomy shortly after Mrs. Ford's operation. An article in the *New York Times Magazine* stated that if Mrs. Ford "achieved nothing else during her husband's Administration, the light her trouble has shed on a dark subject would be contribution enough."[4]

In the weeks following her surgery, Mrs. Ford received, according to White House records, 55,800 cards and messages of good will from the general public. This amounted to ninety-two cubic feet of material, 70 percent of which were printed cards. Perhaps as much as 10 percent of the personal letters came from women who had undergone a similar operation. In a *McCall's* magazine article about the mail she had received, Mrs. Ford wrote that many of the letters "tell a wonderful story of recovery, of appreciation of life, and the magic of love." The following two letters are representative:

> A nurse I met at the hospital when I had this surgery done, and who had also had a mastectomy, said, "This operation makes us stronger women than we were before," and I have found her words to be true! Not only does the air smell sweeter, and flowers look more beautiful, and blue skies more vibrant, but one is able to sort out the unimportant from the important, and needless worries become a thing of the past.
>
> My husband and I (our ages are the same as yours and the President's) had been married 28 years when I was operated on. The trauma of a mastectomy is not in the surgery, but in the psychological doubts women feel—wondering whether their relationship will be altered. Let me assure you that it won't be. Our relationship is strong, beautiful and knit with years of understanding and devotion. A mere mastectomy doesn't change a good marriage except perhaps to add to the closeness.[5]

In the case of her cancer surgery, and her post-administration revelations regarding her alcohol and prescription drug dependencies, Mrs. Ford chose to turn her own misfortune into something positive, the chance to help others.

As soon as she had recovered sufficiently from her surgery, Mrs. Ford resumed her hectic schedule of receptions, "drop-by" appearances, state dinners, and trips. The files of Sheila Weidenfeld, Mrs. Ford's press secretary, are made up of about fifty-two thousand pages of press clippings, background briefing papers, memorandums, and correspondence documenting daily events on Mrs. Ford's calendar; visits of foreign dignitaries; trip arrangements and press coverage; and administrative matters. Folders bearing the following titles indicate just a few of the events in the month of December 1974: "United Cerebral Palsy Poster Children," "Scouter of the Year Dinner," "Christmas Tree Arrival," "People's Republic of China Archaeological Exhibit," "Press Preview of Christmas Decorations," "1975 March of Dimes Poster Child," "Diplomatic Children's Christmas Party," and "White House Christmas Party."

Most of the social events Mrs. Ford took part in required little more than her natural warmth and charm to be successful. However, the White House Central Files contain records of visits with wives of heads of foreign governments for which background briefings were considered necessary. For example, before Mrs. Imelda Marcos came to the White House in November 1975, Mrs. Ford received a three-page memorandum containing background information and suggested topics of conversation. Mrs. Ford was informed that "Mrs. Marcos is noted for her tremendous energy, growing political and financial power, and striking beauty." She was advised to bring up the population crisis, since Mrs. Marcos was in Washington to speak at a conference on that subject, and to say: "I am delighted to see that we both agree on the necessity to speak frankly and candidly on such issues, even if it means we may be criticized. I admire your honesty."[6]

Of the ceremonial events, Mrs. Ford got most involved in planning state dinners and Christmas activities. Here she was able to promote her interest in American arts and crafts and borrowed examples of American artworks from major museums around the country to use as centerpieces. She decorated the White House Christmas tree with ornaments made by the staff of Colonial Williamsburg and had special brochures that contained instructions for making some of the items distributed as Christmas greetings.

In her appearances and interviews, Mrs. Ford generally confined her comments to what she considered "women's issues." One such topic, which was also a political hot potato, was the Equal Rights Amendment. Several state legislatures were scheduled to vote on ratification during 1975. Mrs. Ford arranged to have a slide presentation on the ERA shown in the White House for all staff who could come. The memorandum she sent, which can be found in the White House Central Files, states: "I plan to be on hand to meet you and hope you will bring co-workers for this important briefing. The upcoming year is important to the ratification of the ERA, and I think it's vital to both the men and women who work here to have a clear understanding of the legislation."[7] Her arm-twisting was not limited to the White House staff. She decided to use her influence where it would count most—with the state legislators who would be voting on ratification. She made personal telephone calls to several key individuals in Florida and Illinois. Sheila Weidenfeld's files show that not everyone approved of Mrs. Ford's exercise of free speech. Phyllis Schlafly of "Stop ERA" sent a telegram demanding equal time to present her side of the

Betty Ford was more than an advocate of the ERA. She actively sought support from White House staff and key state legislators.

question to the White House staff and respectfully requested "an accounting of how much federal money has been spent by you and other White House personnel in making long distance calls to legislators, and how much federal money has been spent on salaries of federal employees working for ratification of ERA."[8] An Illinois legislator called Mrs. Ford's actions "demeaning to the stature of the First Lady." Reacting to that, a St. Louis radio station editorial, while against the ERA, stated:

> But we heartily approve of Mrs. Ford's working for passage of ERA or any other political goal. In our opinion, American politics would be strengthened by increased activity by women as office seekers, party leaders and political activists at all levels. This could help our nation shake off its political apathy, and reverse the disgracefully low voter turnout figures. When we start regarding political activity by a first lady, or any citizen, as "demeaning," our democracy is in big trouble. We're going to tell Mrs. Ford how we feel and hope you will too.

And people did tell her. Thirteen cubic feet of mail came into the White House. A lady from New York wrote, "After so many First Ladies who wouldn't go near anything but furniture and gardens, it is truly gratifying to find a woman who is interested in doing a little more for her country."

The opposite side was represented by a letter from Georgia: "Like untold thousands who resent Ms. Ford's attempt to dictate to State Legislatures, it is going to be a genuine joy to vote against any and every Republican that I am privileged to."

Another said simply, "Her intervention on the voting of ERA is an atrocity," while a supporter noted, "This is the first time since Eleanor Roosevelt that a President's wife is coming across as her own person, and a worthwhile person at that." The early mail was predominantly against Mrs. Ford's stand, but when that fact was reported, a wave of supportive mail came in to balance it.

The ERA mail was but a drop in the bucket compared to the deluge Mrs. Ford received in response to her interview with Morley Safer shown on CBS's "60 Minutes" on August 10, 1975. During the two weeks between the taping and the broadcast, no one fully anticipated the tempest it would unleash. Sheila Weidenfeld, in her book *First Lady's Lady*, summed up her feelings about the interview immediately after the taping:

> The substance was good . . . She was open but not outspoken. Honest. She sounded just plain intelligent. The words seemed as legitimate as the smile. Questions were answered thoughtfully, not politically. Abortion, the ups and downs of being a political wife, getting along in marriage, premarital sex. He asked, she answered with a candor rare in a human being, unheard of in a First Lady. I was delighted. So were they. So was she.[9]

A few days before it was aired, Sheila Weidenfeld read the edited transcript checking again for controversy:

> There's a pro-abortion stand; she's said that before. She says she wouldn't be surprised if her children had tried marijuana. She's said that before, too . . . Those words, though—"divorce," "abortion," "marijuana." Definitely shock words. But, I suppose these are shock times. (Would anyone have dared ask Mamie Eisenhower about subjects like that?)[10]

The bombshell turned out to be Mrs. Ford's answer to the question, "What if Susan Ford came to you and said, 'Mother, I'm having an affair?' "

> ***Mrs. Ford:*** Well, I wouldn't be surprised. I think she's a perfectly normal human being like all young girls, if she wanted to continue and I would certainly counsel and advise her on the subject, and I'd want to know pretty much about the young man that she was planning to have the affair with; whether it was a worthwhile encounter or whether it was going to be one of those . . . She's pretty young to start affairs.
> ***Safer:*** But, nevertheless, old enough . . .
> ***Mrs. Ford:*** Oh, yes, she's a big girl.

The next day headlines across the country played up the sensational aspects of the statement, missing Mrs. Ford's intended emphasis that communication should be maintained even if children's attitudes are different from the parents' own. While initial public telephone reaction to the show had been more good than bad, what Sheila Weidenfeld called "the reaction to the reaction," the response to the newspaper stories, was more bad than good.[11] The mail came pouring in!

Mrs. Ford had definitely touched a nerve. People who were for her felt strongly enough to write, especially when they heard about the negative reaction. People who objected to her statements, many of them vehemently, chastised her in no uncertain terms. A few excerpts from the letters illustrate the extent to which Mrs. Ford had truly polarized, and mobilized, the people of the country by talking openly about such controversial subjects:

> You are no lady—first—second or last. Keep your stupid views to yourself from now on.
>
> You not only put your foot in your big mouth, but the other foot and THE MICROPHONE in addition. Maybe you could do a "Nixon" and resign as "First Lady."
>
> Our recent history has seen this nation's First Ladies dedicating themselves to restoring the White House; beautifying America; and remaining silent. You, Mrs. Ford, should take an example from this latter group.

A less emotional, if equally critical, view was expressed by a woman from Cincinnati who wrote:

> Whatever your private feeling regarding the lifestyle of your daughter . . . belongs entirely to you. However, as the wife of the leader of our country and therefore the highest ranking female and mother in the United States, I think your public opinion takes on a different aspect . . . I believe in trying to be honest you thought too narrowly and did not think of the impact on the nation.[12]

Many of the letters expressing support for the first lady mentioned that until they read that the mail was running two to one against her, they had never considered writing, but since someone was keeping score they wanted to be counted. The "pro" letters were generally not as vehement as the "con" letters, but they point out the wide divergence of opinion prevalent in the society.

> How wonderful to hear a contemporary of mine keep abreast of these changing times—be willing to be flexible & be aware that what was once considered right and proper changes from generation to generation. And the intelligent, thinking parent, and adult, should be "open minded" and "aware"—constantly.
>
> Your television debut was fantastic. Whatever you do keep on saying what you think and feel and letting everybody know what a warm, honest and thoroughly intelligent First Lady we have. You are one of the most beautifully contemporary and totally balanced people in public life today.
>
> I cannot understand the criticism as, even though I agreed with all you said, it was refreshing to hear some frank, positive answers instead of wishy-washy dodging of issues as is frequently the case with people in the public eye.

Betty Ford spent most of 1976 traveling and giving short speeches on behalf of her husband. Her appearances were enthusiastically received across the country, and "Betty's Husband for President" buttons and placards proliferated.

> Even if I didn't agree with you, you are as much entitled to your opinions, and entitled to speak them, as any private citizen, and I think the negative response is disgusting and thoroughly uncalled for.

One woman sent a letter-to-the-editor clipped from her local newspaper. It read:

> She's a crusader in the finest tradition of Eleanor Roosevelt. She's as dignified and honest as Bess Truman. She's as elegant as Jacqueline Kennedy. And she's as gracious and perspicacious as Lady Bird Johnson. So who cares if she's married to a Republican?[13]

President Ford told the press that when he heard what his wife had said on "60 Minutes" he figured he had just lost ten million votes, but when he read the newspapers he raised his guess to twenty million. The mail count by October 15 was 10,463 for Mrs. Ford, 23,232 against. But in the long run the polls showed that Mrs. Ford gained significantly in popularity as a result of the controversy. Some people, like the lady who wrote this letter, just liked honesty:

> I am 83 years old, and one of my friends calls me The Last of the Puritans. I haven't been able to decide what our society should do about abortion, and sex relations, and marijuana. But I do know what I think about honesty. I'm for it. And I am deeply grateful that we have someone in the White House who thinks integrity is more important than political advantage. Many thanks for your refreshing example.

When things calmed down a bit, according to Weidenfeld, Mrs. Ford sent Morley Safer her photograph with this inscription, "Morley, if there was anything you forgot to ask . . . I'm grateful."[14]

A weaker person might have become gun-shy after "60 Minutes," but not Mrs. Ford. When it became apparent that she was a political asset and not a liability, the people running President Ford's campaign for reelection sent her out on the campaign trail. She spent most of 1976 traveling and giving short speeches on behalf of her husband in spite of the fact that she had very mixed feelings about spending four more years in the White House. Her appearances were warmly received across the country. "BETTY'S HUSBAND FOR PRESIDENT" buttons and placards proliferated. In Texas, her use of citizen's band radios, a craze of the day, prompted CB enthusiasts to send "First Mama" a total of four cubic feet of mail.

The election, however, went to Jimmy Carter, and Gerald Ford, who had said upon taking office that he was indebted to no man and only one woman, had to ask that woman to read his concession statement because he had laryngitis from last-minute campaigning. On January 20, 1977, Jerry and Betty Ford became private citizens again.

As first lady, Betty Ford filled a unique role. The definitive evaluation of her management of that responsibility ultimately rests with historians. Their judgments will depend, in large part, on the documentary record, a record that is preserved and available in the Gerald R. Ford Library.

Notes

[1]Betty Ford with Chris Chase, *The Times of My Life* (1978), p. 158.

[2]Ibid., p. 120.

[3]Ibid., p. 179.

[4]Jane Howard, "Forward Day by Day," *The New York Times Magazine* 6(Dec. 8, 1974): 36.

[5]"Dear Mrs. Ford . . . ," *McCall's* (Dec. 1974): 64.

[6]Jeanne W. Davis (NSC) to Susan Porter, memo, Nov. 18, 1975, White House Central Files (WHCF), PP5-1, Gerald R. Ford Library, Ann Arbor, MI.

[7]Mrs. Ford to All White House Staff, memo, Feb. 6, 1975, WHCF, PP5-1, GRF Library.

[8]All ERA response letters cited are found in "Women—ERA—Samples & Public Mail," box 7, Weidenfeld Files, GRF Library.

[9]Sheila Rabb Weidenfield, *First Lady's Lady: With the Fords at the White House* (1979), p. 162.

[10]Ibid., p. 168.

[11]Ibid., p. 175.

[12]All letters critical of Mrs. Ford's "60 Minutes" interview are from " '60 Minutes' Bulk Mail Samples," White House Social Files, GRF Library.

[13]All letters supportive of Mrs. Ford's "60 Minutes" interview are from "Columbia Broadcasting System ["60 Minutes" interview with Betty Ford]," box 1, Elizabeth O'Neill Files, GRF Library.

[14]Weidenfeld, *First Lady's Lady*, p. 182.

"These Are Precious Years"

The Papers of Rosalynn Smith Carter

By Faye Lind Jensen

Rosalynn Smith Carter, January 20, 1977. Rosalynn was a serious, hardworking first lady who attended cabinet meetings and high-level briefings during her White House years.

On February 28, 1978, Rosalynn Carter attended her first cabinet meeting. She took notes while "sitting quietly in the background with the other non-Cabinet members."[1] Though her presence at the meetings caused some controversy, it illustrates Mrs. Carter's conscientious interpretation of her role as first lady:

> I was there to be informed so that when I traveled around the country, which I did a great deal, and was questioned by the press and other individuals about all areas of government, I'd know what was going on.[2]

The press and the public were not the only ones interested in Mrs. Carter's feelings on White House policy. Her familiarity with the issues enabled her to be one of Jimmy Carter's most trusted advisers—a role that she had adopted early in their marriage. When visitors to the Carter Museum's "Town Meeting" request information on the couple's relationship, a videotaped image of President Carter responds that he discussed almost every major issue of his presidency with his wife. In 1978 the president revealed that Mrs. Carter frequently edited his speeches. "Rosalynn is able to see things much more clearly, from the viewpoint of the average American, than I am," he said, "So I don't mind her criticizing my speeches."[3]

Keeping abreast of White House policy and acting as a "sounding board" for her husband were but two of the diverse responsibilities that Rosalynn Carter felt were intrinsic to her position. During their first summer in the White House, she served as the president's personal representative on a seven-country tour of Latin America and the Caribbean. With a "fervency" that surprised even her husband, Mrs. Carter acquired a detailed knowledge of each country and its relationship with the United States.[4] She made a list of topics that she intended to discuss with each head of state, touching on such substantive issues as nuclear proliferation, human rights, and economic development. Mrs. Carter's trip obviously made a favorable impression on many Latin Americans and the American public.[5] Shortly after her return, President Carter received a memo from pollster Pat Caddell. Finding that 70 percent of Americans rated the first lady's journey as excellent or good, Caddell concluded that "she clearly helps the President across the board." Before passing the report on to his wife, Jimmy Carter added a handwritten note: "Rosalynn—" he jokingly chided, "don't run against your husband!"[6]

Mrs. Carter continued to serve as the president's emissary throughout his term. In 1979 she and Amy traveled to Italy. Ambassador Dick Gardner reported to the president on Mrs. Carter's visit:

> What the press did not record, however, was the spell which Rosalynn cast on all who met her—from President Pertini, Andreotti, Fanfani at the summit of political powers to the ordinary Italians that saw her (hundreds in person, millions on television) during her tour of Rome.[7]

When neither the president nor vice president could welcome Pope John Paul II to Boston in 1979, Zbigniew Brzezinski requested that President Carter appoint a suitable representative. "The unanimous choice at the working-group level," he wrote, "was—and is—the First Lady." The president agreed.[8]

In her own gracious style, Mrs. Carter enhanced the traditional social role of first lady. Under her direction, the Social Office organized all official and social functions at the White House. In her autobiography, *First Lady From Plains*, Mrs. Carter described the details involved in planning a state visit:

> I was responsible for the arrival ceremony on the South Lawn, the guest list for the dinner, the table decorations, and the entertaining. I was also responsible for planning an interesting schedule for the visiting dignitary's spouse.[9]

In addition to the customary entertainment arranged for White House dinners and receptions, Mrs. Carter organized a Sunday afternoon concert series that featured great performers such as Vladimir Horowitz and Mstislav Rostropovich. The series was broadcast on public television. Mrs. Carter also demonstrated a keen interest in the historical significance of the Executive Mansion. She saw no need for major changes in the house, but did request the restoration of some original furnishings and wallpaper. With the Committee for the Preservation of the White House, she established a White House Trust Fund to procure a permanent collection of American art to replace articles on loan from various individuals and museums.[10]

Mrs. Carter had developed interests and projects while her husband was governor of Georgia, and she had made commitments to various issues during the 1976 campaign. As first lady, she continued and expanded her support of substantive programs like Cities in Schools and improved facilities for the mentally ill. Since the Social Office was competently managed by Gretchen Poston, Mrs. Carter felt that her time and efforts were better spent in helping the American public. "I would not like supervising the entertaining and hospitality, and the domestic running of the White House, to become my main priority," she said in 1978.[11]

Speaking in New York on April 26, 1979, Mrs. Carter described the "awesome responsibility" that she felt accompanied the position of first lady. Explaining that she had the ability to utilize the finest minds in the country and to influence a great number of people, including the president of the United States, she remarked that "these are precious years during which I can contribute."[12] The extent of Mrs. Carter's commitments and contributions is reflected in the files of the first lady's staff.

Mrs. Carter welcomes senior citizens to Activities Day at the White House, September 30, 1978. Rosalynn continues to take an active interest in volunteer work and programs to aid mental health, the community, and the elderly.

The staff was divided into the offices of Social Affairs, Press and Research, Projects and Community Liaison, and Scheduling and Advance. Mrs. Carter also had a "Personal Staff" that included Madeline MacBean, Rita Merthan, and Carol Benefield. In 1978 Press Secretary Mary Finch Hoyt assumed the additional role of "East Wing Coordinator." Kit Dobelle became the director of the East Wing staff in 1979.

The files of the first lady's staff consist of roughly 600,000 pages, which are not currently available for research. The material clearly documents Rosalynn Carter's active role as first lady. The fact that the Projects and Communities File is second in volume only to the Social Office File demonstrates the emphasis she placed on her own work. Directed by Kathy Cade and Jane Fenderson in the Projects and Community Liaison Office, the first lady's staff maintained subject and state files that contain correspondence, reports, and information on Mrs. Carter's involvement with task forces, seminars, committees, and conferences. In the future, researchers will also find a wealth of material in the files of Mrs. Carter's Press Office. In addition to the first lady's speeches, interviews, and press releases, this collection contains fact sheets on her trips and White House events.

Referring to Mrs. Carter's projects, Press Secretary Mary Hoyt once remarked: "Her concerns have enormous breadth. She is working quietly towards a more caring society."[13] Mrs. Carter placed priority on the Equal Rights Amendment, concerns of the elderly, and neighborhood programs. The main thrust of her energy, however, was directed toward mental health programs. Although her Projects File has not been processed, the records of the President's Commission on Mental Health are open for research. Mrs. Carter served as honorary chairperson of the commission, and much of the material contained in this collection was generated by the first lady's staff. The commission held public hearings throughout the nation to investigate the extent of mental illness, its causes and prevention, and the types of treatment and existing facilities. On September 15, 1977, Mrs. Carter commented on the early work of the commission:

> We have held public hearings across the country, and we have listened to the advice and suggestions of hundreds of professionals, lay persons, former mental patients, community organization leaders, and legislators. We have worked up position papers on 24 task panels with the help of more than 200 volunteers. We have worked hard.
>
> And now we have thousands and thousands of pages of data that add up to what I can only describe as a compelling mandate for change. The pages—our interim report—may not be the most spell-binding copy you have ever read. But I urge you to study the evidence.[14]

Transcripts of the commission's meetings and hearings, as well as its final report, are included in this collection.

In April 1978 Mrs. Carter presented the commission's final recommendations to the president, and on May 15, 1979, he submitted the Mental Health Systems Act to Congress for approval. The bill provided for the first overhaul of national mental health policy since 1963. As the first president's wife since Eleanor Roosevelt to testify before Congress, Mrs. Carter appeared before the Senate Subcommittee on Health in support of the act. Mrs. Carter and her staff, along with the president's Domestic Policy Staff, lobbied diligently for the bill. On July 24, 1980, Stuart Eizenstat, the president's chief adviser on domestic issues, was notified that the first lady was prepared to phone Speaker O'Neill "to request expedited floor action . . . before she leaves for Peru on Saturday."[15] The Mental Health Systems Act was approved and funded by Congress in September 1980.

The expansion of duties performed by recent first ladies resulted in the formation of a separate First Family White House Central File, Subject File. The purpose of the system was to provide prompt file service to the first lady and her staff and to handle the increasing amount of correspondence directed to the first family. This unprocessed collection contains over one hundred cubic feet of material. The subject categories are similiar to those in the original White House Central File and will be particularly useful to future researchers. The following two letters illustrate the type of correspondence that is contained in the First Family White House Central File. The first letter was filed under the subject heading "WE-4," which is the subcategory for concerns of the elderly.

> Dear Mrs. Carter,
>
> Bless you for your interest in and concern for America's older citizens.
>
> It is a very terrifying experience getting older in America. You suddenly find yourself an out-sider. Indeed one reaches an age—where one is almost considered not to exist.
>
> A most terrifying and depressing experience.

The following letter was placed in the subject file "FG-287, Federal Government Organizations–President's Commission on Mental Health":

> Dear Mrs. Carter:
>
> As the mother of an emotionally disturbed daughter, I am writing to thank you for your interest and activity in the field of mental health. In the future, I do hope that these individuals will be accepted and treated with the same consideration that other patients receive.
>
> My daughter is 24, very intelligent, creative, and has been ill for five years. The cost of adequate treatment for her is prohibitive. Thus, I want to express my support for some type of national health insurance.
>
> Mrs. Carter, you are an outstanding First Lady and one that American females can emulate. I am proud that you are from the South.[16]

Toward the end of the Carter presidency, Rosalynn Carter devoted a great deal of her time to the reelection campaign. As she noted in her autobiography: "Because of the hostages, Jimmy was staying close to the White House, but I was facing the farmers—and Ted Kennedy—in Iowa."[17] From September 1979 to October 1980, Mrs. Carter visited 166 cities in 39 states. The decision to use her as a "presidential surrogate" was political, as well as practical. Mrs. Carter was able to boast of her husband's virtues and accomplishments in a warm and sincere tone. After hearing her speak in Dallas, Liz Carpenter described the first lady's style: "She talks with great fervor and conveys the message better than anybody because she really believes in him. She's smart and appealing."[18] One reporter described Mrs. Carter as "one of the most effective stand-up campaigners in the country."[19] When her papers are open, researchers will find a large amount of material on Mrs. Carter's campaigning in the files of her Press Office, Scheduling and Advance Office, and in the Trip File of personal secretary Rita Merthan.

Mrs. Carter interrupted her early campaign efforts in the fall of 1979 to support yet another cause. On November 9, she accompanied a group of experts to the Cambodian refugee camps in Thailand. "Nothing," she reflected, "had prepared me for the human suffering I saw in the refugee camps when I arrived."[20] Mrs. Carter met with the king of Thailand and then returned home to rally support for improving conditions for the Cambodians. Her trip spurred the organization of the National Cambodian Crisis Committee and the Cambodian Crisis Center. The first lady also made public television appearances to appeal for aid from the American people. The television spots and Mrs. Carter's discussion of the refugees on the "Today Show" are part of the audiovisual holdings of the Jimmy Carter Library and are available to researchers.[21]

Rosalynn, 18, and Jimmy Carter, 21, on their wedding day, July 7, 1946. Only Eliza McCardle Johnson married at a younger age among first ladies.

Though the papers of the First Lady's Staff and the First Family White House Central File are not available at this time, there are files open for research at the Jimmy Carter Library that contain material about Rosalynn Carter. The original White House Central File, Subject File is available, and the Subject Code "PP 5-1 (Carter, Rosalynn)" contains about two thousand pages. Papers in this file relate to Mrs. Carter's trips, her work on mental health, and social affairs at the White House. There is one item that illustrates Mrs. Carter's involvement in political policy, particularly when it concerned her husband's public image. On August 7, 1979, novelist Allen Drury bitterly attacked the president in a *New York Times* editorial. In the following note to Press Secretary Jody Powell, the first lady suggests a White House response.

> Jody-
> I think we should demand equal time with NY Times Op. Ed. articles. After Allan [*sic*] Drury–and another either Sun. or Mon. I don't see how they can refuse. We could get Sol Linowitz or someone supportive to write.
> R.[22]

There are also references to the first lady scattered throughout the office files of the president's staff. For instance, Jody Powell's files contain press releases of the question and answer sessions that Mrs. Carter held during her trip to

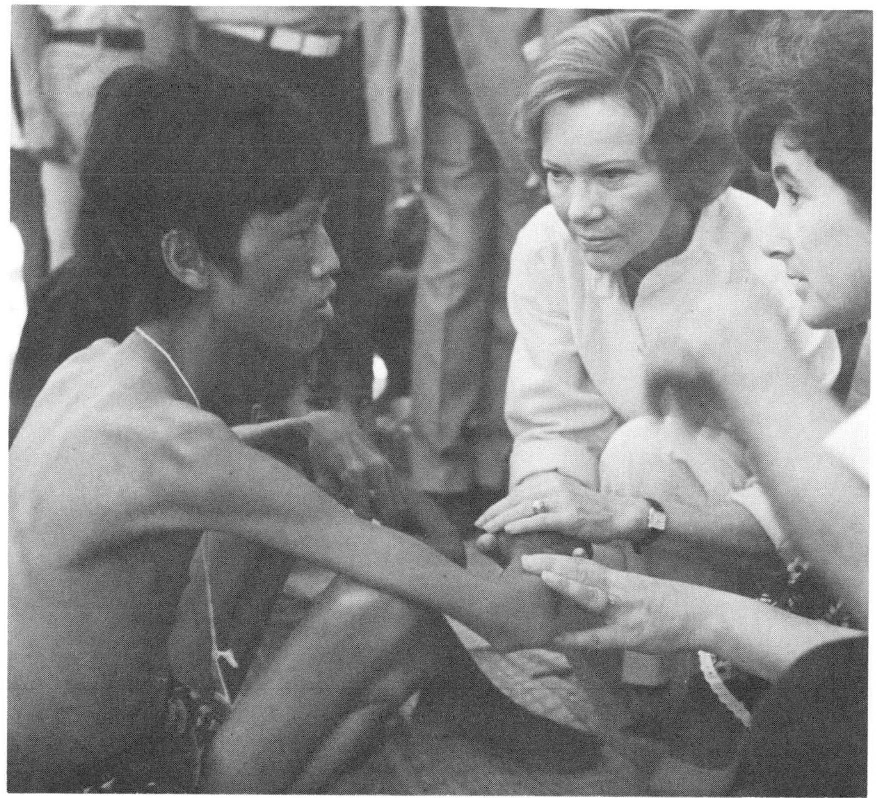

Mrs. Carter visited Cambodian refugees in Thailand during fall 1979. "Nothing," she said, "had prepared me for the human suffering I saw in the refugee camps when I arrived."

Latin America. In the files of Sarah Weddington, Special Assistant for Women's Affairs, there is a printed pro-ERA speech that Mrs. Carter delivered in New York City on April 26, 1979. The Office of Administration Files contain information on Mrs. Carter's travel and allocation of time. A press release in this collection outlines the first lady's activities for September 1979. White House events during that month included an "Old Fashioned Gospel Singin'" on the South Lawn, a reception for the Archbishop of the Greek Orthodox Church, and a state dinner for Mexican President Lopez Portillo. Mrs. Carter also held receptions for the Coalition of National Voluntary Organizations, women of the Congressional Black Caucus, and the board members of the National Symphony Orchestra. Events outside the White House took the first lady to a coffee with senior citizens, a discussion of home heating oil, and a museum opening. She also spent six days campaigning.[23]

Mrs. Carter's departure from the White House did not bring an end to her activism. After completing her autobiography in 1984, she co-authored a book with President Carter titled *Everything to Gain.* The book gives an account of the Carters' life since they left Washington and offers their views on health and activity during retirement. Since 1981 Mrs. Carter has served on the board of directors for the National Association of Mental Health and as honorary chairperson of the Friendship Force exchange program. She is a popular speaker on mental health and women's issues. She and the president are active participants in the Habitat for Humanity housing organization, the Task Force for Child Survival, and other humanitarian efforts. Mrs. Carter has participated in numerous symposiums and has sponsored conferences at the Carter Center and Emory University. Her postpresidential correspondence and scheduling files are housed at the Carter Library and will be available for future research.

Rosalynn Carter has emerged as one of the most industrious and influential women ever to have inhabited the White House. Weekly working lunches with the president, attendance at cabinet meetings, involvement in campaign strategy sessions—such actions occasionally created public rumblings about a first lady who wielded excessive power. The press also found fault with Mrs. Carter's selection of projects. It seems that mental health was not "sexy" enough to attract extensive coverage. But Mrs. Carter was simply acting out a role that came naturally. "I feel very comfortable in what I'm doing," she once said. "And I'm accomplishing something. And that's important."[24]

Notes

[1]Rosalynn Carter, *First Lady From Plains* (1984), p. 176.

[2]Ibid., p. 176.

[3]Desmond Wilcox, "Americans—Rosalynn Carter: The First Lady," *Book Digest* (Apr. 1978): 49.

[4]Ibid., p. 46.

[5]Bob Pastor to Jody Powell and Jerry Schecter, memo, Oct. 18, 1977, PP 5-1 Ex., box PP-3, Subject File, White House Central File (WHCF), Jimmy Carter Library, Atlanta, GA.

[6]Pat Caddell to President Carter, memo, July 30, 1977, "Memoranda: First Lady's Staff, 2/2/78–10/2/78 [CF O/A 160]," box 42, Jody Powell's Files, White House Staff Office Files, JC Library.

[7]Dick Gardner to President Carter, May 11, 1979, PP 5-1 Ex., box PP-3, Subject File, WHCF, JC Library.

[8]Zbigniew Brzezinski to President Carter, memo, Sept. 17, 1979, PP 5-1 Ex., box PP-3, Subject File, WHCF, JC Library.

[9]Carter, *First Lady From Plains*, p. 219.

[10]Ibid., pp. 156–157, 217.

[11]Wilcox, "Americans–Rosalynn Carter," pp. 43–45.

[12]Printed speech, Apr. 26, 1979, in "Women and America, Rosalynn Carter Challenges America," box 44, Sarah Weddington's Files, White House Staff Office Files, JC Library.

[13]Joy Billington, "Press Aide Mary Hoyt Says First Lady Can't be Labelled," *Washington Star*, Apr. 23, 1978, p. D-3.

[14]Press release, "Washington Press Club–Mrs. Carter's Remarks," Sept. 15, 1977, box 25, Records of President's Commission on Mental Health, RG 220, JC Library.

[15]Jim Mongan and Tony Imler to Stuart Eizenstat, memo, July 24, 1980, attached to Stuart Eizenstat to Congressman Henry Waxman, memo, May 14, 1980, HE 1-4 Ex., box HE-5, Subject File, WHCF, JC Library.

[16]Both letters are from the "Partner of the President" exhibit in the Museum of the Jimmy Carter Library, Atlanta, GA.

[17]Carter, *First Lady from Plains*, p. 315.

[18]"Woman Behind the Throne Woos Votes in Revere," *Boston Herald American*, Feb. 15, 1980.

[19]Jurate Kazickas, ". . . The First Lady is a Hit on the Hustings," *Washington Star*, July 26, 1979, p. D-1.

[20]Carter, *First Lady From Plains*, p. 295.

[21]The records of the Cambodian Crisis Committee are in the University of Notre Dame Archives, Notre Dame, IN.

[22]Rosalynn Carter to Jody Powell, memo, n.d., attached to Madeline MacBean to Jody Powell, memo, Aug. 15, 1979, PP 5-1 Ex., box PP-3, Subject File, WHCF, JC Library.

[23]Press release, Office of the First Lady's Press Secretary, Sept. 5, 1979, "First Lady's Office," box 29, Hugh Carter's Files, White House Staff Office Files, JC Library.

[24]Vicki Pearlman, "Rosalynn: A Portrait of the First Lady," *Atlanta Journal*, Oct. 30, 1978, p. 21A.

"She Saves Everything"
The Papers of Nancy Davis Reagan

By Carl Sferrazza Anthony

Dedicated to a domestic role and support of her husband, Nancy Davis Reagan has also helped wage the battle against teenage drug abuse in America.

Nineteen eighty-nine, the year of the bicentennial of the American presidency, marks another important, but less recognized anniversary, that of the first ladyship. On January 20 of that year, another historic milestone will be turned with the departure of Nancy Davis Reagan from that "office."

She will become one of those few among her predecessors to have served for two terms—eight full years—in the White House, joining the ranks of Martha Washington, Dolley Madison, Elizabeth Monroe, Julia Grant, Eleanor Roosevelt, and Mamie Eisenhower. With the possible exception of Eleanor Roosevelt, who was in the White House for twelve years, Mrs. Reagan's public and private papers will almost certainly be the most voluminous of all the first ladies.

Because Mrs. Reagan has served at a time in history when mass communication is capable of instantly transmitting a first lady's image by television and capturing it through the replay capabilities of videotape, the public has become acutely aware of her activities. Mrs. Reagan's tenure has been documented by regular, often weekly, coverage on the national television networks, as well as by local news programs. Equally important is the fact that, more than most presidential couples, the Reagans have made many joint appearances. This in turn has served as a catalyst for an increase in the public mail response to their activities.

Another factor in the great public interest in Mrs. Reagan is her concern about the problem of drug abuse among the young. It has been a particularly timely, and occasionally controversial, topic of general debate throughout the 1980s. Just as Jacqueline Kennedy's White House restoration came at a time when historic preservation was gaining in popularity, and Lady Bird Johnson's beautification program expanded the environmental movement of the 1960s, Mrs. Reagan's work against drug abuse parallels the great concern and interest shown by government, the press—in fact, the international community.

The growing problem of drugs is linked to larger and diverse political issues such as international narcotics smuggling, civil liberties of drug-tested employees in both the public and private sectors of the national workforce, highway fatalities, AIDS, and economic dependence of third world countries on drug exports. Nancy Reagan began raising public consciousness on drug abuse prevention early in the decade and has become closely associated with that subject.

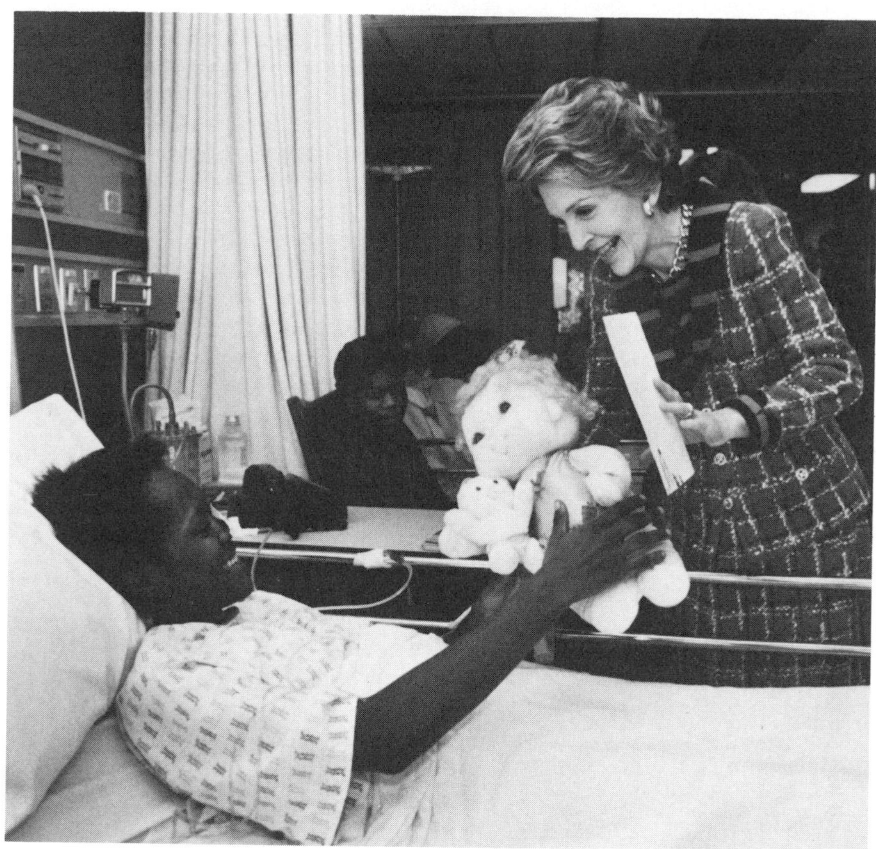

Nancy Reagan left the glitter of Hollywood "to be the wife I wanted to be." Home and family are top priorities for Mrs. Reagan, and her work with children, the elderly, and numerous charitable organizations has endeared the first lady to all Americans.

Nowhere is there better proof of this than in the enormous volume of mail that she receives on the issue. Betty Ford once said that if the West Wing is the mind of the nation, then the East Wing—the first lady's bailiwick—is its heart. With Mrs. Reagan's highly visible work on drug abuse and prevention, her East Wing office has become something of a national information clearing house on this issue, attracting thousands of letters from across the country and around the world requesting and offering advice, opinions, and personal stories.

There is also a more personal reason to believe that the archival holdings documenting this first lady will be voluminous. In the words of one staff member, Deputy Press Secretary Betsy Koons, "She saves everything." Like the office files of Jacqueline Kennedy, who requested that all her records be kept, it is likely that Nancy Reagan's papers will be extremely thorough. Many have pointed out that she is interested in her husband's place in history, but few have noted that she is equally aware of her own contributions.

During her first few months "in office," Mrs. Reagan made a conscious effort to learn more about her predecessors. Her reading list included Sylvia Morris's biography of Edith Carow Roosevelt, the wife of Theodore Roosevelt, and she also was fascinated by Frances Wright Saunders's biography of Ellen Axson Wilson, the first wife of Woodrow Wilson.[1] In addition, Mrs. Reagan discussed various aspects of her role with some of her recent predecessors. With Jacqueline Kennedy Onassis she considered the press criticism that comes along with the position; with Pat Nixon she discussed her own upcoming activities in a planned visit to China.[2]

Her sense of history also extends to her husband's papers, however incidental. In the harrowing days following the March 1981 assassination attempt on President Reagan, several slips of notepaper on which he had penned jokes and questions were discovered to be missing. Michael K. Deaver, the president's deputy chief of staff, recalled that staff members had "lifted" three of the notes, and "threats had to be made before they were turned in." Other notes were never found, perhaps becoming valuable souvenirs for some of the hospital staff. Those that were retrieved were given to Mrs. Reagan for safekeeping. "They will become an exhibit when a Ronald Reagan Library is built," wrote Deaver, "priceless, historical quips, written in the dawn after a dark night."[3]

Not only Mrs. Reagan but also her staff have been scrupulous in retaining records of all sorts that document Mrs. Reagan's activities. The press office, in particular, has diligently retained every piece of printed material—regardless of its slant. Elaine Crispen, press secretary to the first lady, commented that the staff regularly boxes up files and clippings for transfer to the White House Central Files unit. Betsy Schaben, director of first lady correspondence, noted that there is very little space in the East Wing to store the office's files, and in fact, what documents kept there are stored in flat files.

Just exactly what would a researcher find in the records of the Nancy Reagan years? Though it will be some time before National Archives staff will be able to appraise the mountain of material, and then to arrange, describe, and make these documents available for public examination, certain documentation can be anticipated. Certainly the Reagan Papers will include the routine materials found in all first ladies' collections—social files, press releases, and public mail. Yet, Mrs. Reagan's collections also promise some unique data.

First ladies often reflect the moods and concerns of their generation. Mamie Eisenhower was indicative of many American women her age in the 1950s. Betty Ford's involvement in the women's movement and open discussion of changing morals seemed quite the mainstream for the 1970s. Mrs. Reagan's traditional devotion to her husband, her simultaneous devotion to her own job, and her involvement in the fight against drug abuse all seem to reflect the lifestyle of mature American women with both careers and family. Though the first lady herself has said that she has not changed to suit her position, perhaps the times in which she has served changed and suited her. Whatever the case, she grew into the job. Bill Barol of *Newsweek* has pointed out that "Decades are not a function of calendar time. They are trends, values and associations, bundled up and tied together in the national memory." Barol believes that Ronald Reagan "was the embodiment of the 80's," and that Mrs. Reagan's work on drug abuse helped "to open a tap in the national consciousness."[4]

In terms of Mrs. Reagan's work, and what will likely be found in her office files, such a declaration is particularly relevant. In these materials there will be a particularly thorough record of the drug abuse debate.[5] A very large portion of Mrs. Reagan's public mail relates to her drug abuse project work. Mail to Mrs. Reagan from around the world touches on all aspects of the drug abuse epidemic and ranges from reports on technical substance abuse studies to poignant requests for help from drug abusers.

The amount of Mrs. Reagan's public mail is impressive. In 1981 she received 78,803 letters; 1982, 37,670; 1983, 39,982; 1984, 44,871; 1985, 54,463; 1986, 61,074; and in 1987, 85,930. As the first lady's visibility has increased over the years, so too has the amount of correspondence. Although a specific breakdown of issues within these figures is not available, Elaine Crispen notes that drug abuse and appeals for personal assistance are the most frequently addressed topics.[6]

The 1981 assassination attempt on the president and the first lady's 1987 mastectomy represent peak public mail periods. The volume of mail to Mrs. Reagan rose dramatically during various crises and events of the Reagan administration. Virtually every letter sent to Mrs. Reagan receives a reply, and she personally reads a representative sample of the many letters she receives.

Whenever there have been controversial public issues in different historical eras, first ladies received mail about it–from Lucy Hayes and the Mormon practice of polygamy in the 1870s to Lady Bird Johnson and the war in Vietnam in the 1960s. Along these lines, Mrs. Reagan's public mail also reflects such typical issues of the 1980s as the AIDS crisis, deficit reduction, and the Iran-Contra affair.

The documentation of Mrs. Reagan's personal appearances also will be of value to historians and presidential researchers. As one of the first lady's speechwriters, I was able to get a look into the workings of the East Wing. From personal experience I know that materials used in the preparation of Mrs. Reagan's speeches were routinely preserved in her Special Project Files. A typical file will include an invitation from a group or organization to the first lady plus documentation on a decision to accept the invitation. The steps from initial request through final speech generally followed a set pattern.

About a month before a scheduled event, the special projects director would turn over the event file to a speechwriter. The next step was for the special projects director and the first lady's chief of staff to brief the speechwriter on the details of the event. Was it to be an audience of adults or children? How long should the speech run? What chord should be struck—emotional, casual, or informational? Notes on these briefings may be found in the Special Project Files, though I cannot be certain how other speechwriters kept their notes.

These event files will document the message Mrs. Reagan has taken to parents, students, and teachers on organizing local programs against drug abuse. A national network of groups has emerged as a direct result of the first lady's speaking out on the issue, the most familiar being the "Just Say No" youth clubs. Many of the letters to Mrs. Reagan open with references to seeing the first lady on television, hearing her on the radio, or reading a newspaper story about her drug abuse campaign. These personal letters may provide future historians with insights not only into Mrs. Reagan's career, but also into the drug problem of the 1980s. Judging from the many appearances she has made and the length of time she has been first lady, Mrs. Reagan's Special Projects Files will be voluminous. Because she has been in office for eight years, and began making public appearances right from the start, it is probably true that Mrs. Reagan has delivered more public speeches than any other first lady since Eleanor Roosevelt. Nancy Reagan makes an average of three dozen speeches a year, and has traveled to sixty-four different cities in thirty-three states, in the majority of cases to address the issue of drug abuse.

Historians will have to do research in other files, such as the press clippings files, to ensure the accuracy of the information in the Special Project Files. Though the speech may have been approved by the first lady and exists in the file for the event, it may never have been delivered because the first lady sometimes decides to speak extemporaneously. Besides fact-checking in the press clippings, however, there will be another unique research tool for future historians studying the vast video and still picture collection created by the first lady's staff.

The proliferation of videotape in the 1980s generated a new and rich communication medium. No longer are bulky cameras and lights necessary to record public events. No longer are copies of television news and special reports available only by the tedious process of reel-to-reel film. Because of her many appearances on prime-time television, and network and local news coverage of

In June 1985, President and Mrs. Reagan attended a fundraiser for the John F. Kennedy Library where the first lady shared a smile with former first lady Jacqueline Kennedy.

her activities, Nancy Reagan's public appearances as first lady will be thoroughly documented. Not only do the networks send videotapes to the White House, but also the first lady's staff members occasionally use video machines at home to record Mrs. Reagan's appearances.

In addition to the videotapes, there is also a vast collection of still photographs documenting Mrs. Reagan's career at both solo appearances and those she makes with the president. For each event there are often several dozen photographs taken by one of the official White House photographers. The press office possesses a large library of books of the contact sheets of White House photographs catalogued by date and event. There is also Mrs. Reagan's own vast collection of personal photographs, many of which are now displayed throughout the family quarters and in her personal office in the mansion.[7]

Mrs. Reagan's Social Files, which incorporate state and official dinner guest lists, entertainments, and menus, have been retained just as those from previous administrations have been kept. What may make them unique, however, is that they, more than any other files of the first lady's office, reflect both Reagans' early careers as actors. White House guests are regularly drawn from the entertainment profession, and lists include names like Mary Martin, Jimmy Stewart, Elizabeth Taylor, and John Travolta among many others. State dinner entertainment has generally reflected the first lady's personal taste, as well as her consideration for the likes and dislikes of the guest of honor. "Mrs. Reagan is extremely concerned and involved with all the performing artists," said Muffy Brandon, the first Reagan social secretary.[8]

Like Lady Bird Johnson, Nancy Reagan keeps a White House diary. Unlike Mrs. Johnson, who spoke her day's thoughts into a tape recorder, Mrs. Reagan maintains a handwritten diary. Mrs. Reagan plans to publish her memoirs, though it is uncertain whether the published form will contain only excerpts of her diary as Mrs. Johnson's did. Surely the full diaries will someday be available for future generations of scholars. Like the unpublished notes and drafts of Edith Bolling Wilson's autobiography—only part of which she used in the published version—a full diary account of the first lady's recollections of eight years should prove invaluable to future generations and provide personal insights into a tumultuous era in American history.

To what extent Mrs. Reagan has kept copies of her handwritten letters is unknown, but copies of special letters of which carbons were not made might also be found among her personal papers. Undoubtedly, such historical exchanges as those between Mrs. Reagan and Raisa Gorbachev will include photocopies of Mrs. Reagan's letters. Perhaps, as in Lady Bird Johnson's papers, there will be a "Special Persons" correspondence file.

In terms of her political interest in her husband's administration, Mrs. Reagan has worked with a large number of presidential aides. Unlike past first ladies, however, most of her contact with the president's staff has been by telephone rather than by memorandum. This was true with Michael Deaver,

Always hard at work, Nancy Reagan has shared her interest in the arts by using the Executive Mansion as a showcase for young performers on PBS television. During her first year in the White House, the first lady directed major renovations of the second- and third-floor quarters.

deputy chief of staff, and later with Chief of Staff Donald Regan. Telephone logs reflect the date, time, and the length of calls, but they do not provide information on the nature of the discussions. Any memorandums, briefing or informational papers that were directed to the West Wing from the East Wing, however, should show up in the papers of the president's advisers. In this respect, it is very likely that future historians will find much relating to Mrs. Reagan in the files of Michael Deaver while he served as deputy chief of staff to the president.

Mrs. Reagan's office, like those of other recent first ladies, routinely directs certain requests from the public to various government departments and agencies. Copies of the correspondence, official requests for federal action, and the results of the request are all retained in White House Correspondence Files. It is likely that evidence of government action prompted by Mrs. Reagan's office will be found in the collections of various administration officials. Along these lines, it is important to remember that all White House mail has been categorized and filed by the name of the letter writer, not the name of the addressee.

Perhaps one of the greatest resources among the records of the first lady is the wide-reaching and diverse press-clipping collection maintained by the press office. What makes it particularly important is that there was, and is, no attempt to screen any editorials or articles that might be critical of the first lady. As Deputy Press Secretary Betsy Koons notes, "Every time Mrs. Reagan's name appears in a story or article it's clipped and kept for the files."

The press generated by the first lady, in combination with the fact that she has been in her position for a relatively long tenure, will make this collection particularly helpful in many respects. Not only will it be valuable as a source for fact- and date-checking, it also will be useful in tracing the changing attitudes of reporters and other journalists covering Mrs. Reagan from 1981 to 1989. Of related interest are the files of the press office, which maintain records of journalists' and other writers' requests for information and interviews. Such a permanent record may reflect on the growing national interest in first ladies generally, and Mrs. Reagan specifically.

How much of Mrs. Reagan's pre-White House papers will be in the future Reagan Library? What about school essays and family letters? Will the papers of her mother, Edith Davis, become part of the collection? Will there be press clippings, film and stage scripts, studio publicity press releases of Mrs. Reagan's own film and stage career? It is probable—since Mrs. Reagan does keep important mementos—but it is not certain how much will end up in the Reagan Library. An item like an old family photograph album of Mrs. Reagan's childhood years will most certainly be included in a future pre-White House collection. Letters between the president and Mrs. Reagan before their marriage will probably be sparse, since they both lived in Hollywood and were rarely separated while they were engaged and married.

Living in the White House for as long as she has, and being so conscious of her own role, Nancy Reagan will surely leave vast records encompassing a multitude of issues, activities, and perspectives of one of the most vivid eras of the late twentieth century.

Notes

The author wishes to acknowledge the assistance of Elaine Crispen, press secretary; Betsy Koons, deputy press secretary; Wendy Weber Toler, deputy press secretary; Linda Faulkner, social secretary to the White House; and Betsy Schaben, director of first lady correspondence. Special thanks to Mrs. Ronald Reagan, who offered suggestions and corrections.

[1]Nancy Reagan to author, Oct. 29, 1985.

[2]Michael K. Deaver, *Behind the Scenes*, (1988), p. 118.

[3]Deaver, *Behind the Scenes*, p. 23.

[4]Bill Barol, "The Eighties Are Over," *Newsweek*, Jan. 4, 1988, pp. 40, 41.

[5]Ibid., p. 43.

[6]It is interesting to note that requests for personal assistance also accounted for a large percentage of Martha Washington's public mail. For nearly two hundred years, such appeals have continued to be among the most frequent requests, proving in some respects that with the first ladyship, the more some elements of the role change, the more they stay the same.

[7]Jerrold M. Packard, *American Monarchy, A Social Guide to the Presidency*, (1983), p. 33–34.

[8]Elise K. Kirk, *Music at the White House*, (1986), p. 355.

AFTERWORD

The Historical Legacy of Modern First Ladies

During the past decade, the perennial American fascination with first ladies has recently given signs of achieving a new level of intensity. In 1982 a poll of scholars rated all the presidential wives for the first time, just as their husbands have been periodically evaluated. Eleanor Roosevelt, Abigail Adams, and Lady Bird Johnson led the list, in that order. Two years later, in April 1984, a conference at the Gerald R. Ford Museum, sponsored by Betty Ford, examined "Modern First Ladies: Private Lives and Public Duties." Media coverage was lavish, with dozens of national reporters and the major networks in attendance. Rosalynn Carter's autobiography, *First Lady From Plains*, outsold Jimmy Carter's memoirs and became the leading bestseller in paperback. By the summer of 1985, Nancy Reagan received an hour of prime-time attention when NBC ran a special on "The First Lady: Nancy Reagan," which described her triumph over the early criticism of her stylish and expensive way of life. Fred Barnes in the *New Republic* credited her with "one of the greatest political turnabouts in modern times."

Popular curiosity about first ladies—and analysis of their performance—is, of course, a continuing aspect of American life. In August 1861 the *Chicago Tribune* complained about the way rival newspapers were treating Mary Todd Lincoln. "If Mrs. Lincoln were a prize fighter, a foreign danseuse, or a condemned convict on the way to execution, she could not be treated more indecently than she is by a portion of the New York press." Lucy Webb Hayes, one of the first women to be called first lady, received letters regularly from the public that asked her among other things to discuss polygamy or to allow seances to be conducted at the White House. Grover Cleveland experienced the insatiable lust for gossip about presidents and their wives when, while in the White House, in 1886, he married Frances Folsom.

Despite the long tradition of first lady watching, efforts to understand this singularly American institution in its historical context have been rare. Journalists and pundits write about each new president and his wife as if there were few previous examples with which to compare accomplishments and style. An NBC producer described Mrs. Reagan's relationship as counselor and adviser to the president as "unique," without any recognition that Edith Roosevelt, Helen Taft, and Bess Truman were all closer to their husbands than Mrs. Reagan on personnel and policy decisions. More important, almost no efforts have been

Mamie Eisenhower's outgoing manner, her love of pretty clothes and jewelry, and her pride in husband and home enhanced the popularity of this first lady during the 1950s.

made to determine why first ladies captivate the public or to measure the ways in which the relationship between these women and the American people has evolved in this century.

That first ladies have emerged since 1900 as public figures in their own right is a cliche often repeated in the small body of literature about them. The real issue is the quality of their participation in national affairs. Treating them in a feminist context is unproductive because over the years they have so well reflected and exemplified middle-class family values. To characterize first ladies as partners or surrogates of the president conveys only a part of the truth. They are best understood as a variety of political celebrity, and the complexities of their situation arise from the imperatives and constraints that accompany stardom and celebrity status in American society.

The continuing question for all first ladies has been how to come to terms with this unrelenting attention—"having every move watched and covered and considered news," in the words of Lady Bird Johnson. Some women have found the demands of celebrity status beyond their strength and the pressures too great. Helen Taft, Ellen Wilson, and Florence Harding suffered debilitating health problems in the White House, and Mamie Eisenhower, Patricia Nixon, and Betty Ford showed the strain as well.

For the most part, however, modern first ladies have developed the means to gratify or accommodate what a biographer of Jacqueline Kennedy Onassis calls "the squeezing paw of the public." In the first thirty years of this century, journalistic techniques and practices remained tentative and unsophisticated. Edith Roosevelt, Grace Coolidge, and Lou Henry Hoover explored some of the possibilities that were open to a presidential wife to find a place for herself as a public personality, but Edith Wilson's example provided a cautionary warning about a first lady who brushed too close to substance.

While Edith Roosevelt enjoyed the confidence of her husband on matters of appointments and probably influenced policy during their daily walks in the White House gardens, it was her position as a symbol of what American women should be that represented her most important public role.

Under the Roosevelts, the White House became "the recognized leader of Washington official society." Edith Roosevelt first asserted her cultural preeminence through regular weekly meetings of Cabinet wives, which resulted in what one reporter called "several wise reformations" in social affairs. "I know the veneration the Americans have for the office of the Presidency," Mrs. Roosevelt said, "and I feel that, as far as possible, they should meet their Chief Executive and see the way in which he lives." Mrs. Roosevelt made these remarks to a reporter doing a story on her "social duties," which was itself a further departure from the private wall that had previously separated the first ladies from the public. Mrs. Roosevelt never flouted the social code that kept first ladies out of public view, but she found ways that a president's wife might use her fame to make the White House a force in what an aide to Theodore Roosevelt called "the moral social life of America."

Although she lacked any of Mrs. Roosevelt's influence on her husband's policy decisions, Grace Coolidge capitalized on the public's curiosity about her activities as a patron of culture and friend of the famous in the 1920s. Photogenic and well dressed, Mrs. Coolidge became a favorite of the press as a contrast to

A near-perfect hostess, the multilingual Jacqueline Bouvier Kennedy welcomes members of the diplomatic corps to the White House for tea.

her dour and distant husband. A full schedule of receptions and musicales brought the celebrated and talented to the White House, among them Douglas Fairbanks, John Barrymore, and Sergei Rachmaninoff. Calvin Coolidge may have forbidden her to make any statements, speak on the radio, or smoke in public, but at the same time he knew that a glamorous and attractive first lady added an aura of sophistication and fun to an otherwise austere administration.

Even such an apparently reclusive woman as Lou Henry Hoover was actually more in the public gaze than her reputation would indicate. She made a number of nationwide radio broadcasts and was available to the press informally on her trips, while asserting each time that she gave no interviews. The size of her personal staff grew to three secretaries to cope with the increase in mail that her expanded public activities evoked.

Other first ladies in the early 1900s tried to balance the demands of fame with impulses to be a larger force in the lives of their husbands. Helen Taft had what she termed "a lively interest" in William Howard Taft's political career. After inducing him to run for president in 1908, she advised him on Cabinet appointments and diplomatic nominations. Her public visibility, however, caused troubles in the transition period and in the early weeks of her husband's administration. Mrs. Taft expressed the desire, even before her husband took over from Theodore Roosevelt, to redecorate the White House and make changes in the staff. The resulting friction with the Roosevelts contributed to the feud that, in turn, led to disaster for the Republicans in 1912. Had Mrs. Taft not suffered a crippling illness in the spring of 1909, her energy and sense of her own position would have tested the limits of what first ladies might do as public figures.

Illness also limited the influence of Florence Harding and Ellen Wilson as first ladies, but their brief stays in the White House disclose how presidential wives both responded to public attention and sought to evoke it. Mrs. Harding threw open the White House mansion to the people after the long exclusion during World War I and Woodrow Wilson's illness. She met tourists personally and once greeted a contingent of Girl Scouts in a Girl Scout uniform of her own. After a long bout with ill health in 1922, she invited women reporters to tea to see how she had recovered. This effort to quell apprehension about Mrs. Harding's health reflected the news value that a celebrity-conscious press assigned to the intimate details of White House life.

Woodrow Wilson's first wife, Ellen Axson Wilson, might seem an improbable candidate for celebrity status. In her seventeen months in Washington, she avoided direct publicity, but she and her husband managed to make their social presence known through other means. Giving frugality and economy as their reasons, the Wilsons declined to hold an inaugural ball in 1913, and the first lady also let it be known that she spent under a thousand dollars a year on clothes. The Wilsons matched this "Democratic simplicity" with numerous disclosures about their family activities that consistently had news coverage. "One gets tired of seeing, hearing, and talking Wilsons," wrote a congressional wife. "They are more before the public than any other White House family I have known." Mrs. Wilson used her public visibility to advocate a law to clean up Washington's disease-infested and overcrowded alleys. Congress passed the measure just before her death in partial recognition that the popularity of a first lady could give her an influence on questions of public policy.

Edith Bolling Wilson, who married the president in December 1915, achieved a different kind of notoriety when her husband suffered a disabling stroke in October 1919. Historians still call her a "President-in-fact" who, in James Reston's words, assumed Wilson's "Presidential responsibilities." These judgments overstate the extent of Mrs. Wilson's influence from late 1919 to March 4, 1921. But the first lady controlled who saw President Wilson in the negotiations over the Senate ratification of the Treaty of Versailles, and she had a large influence upon her husband in his dealings with such former advisers as Edward M. House and Secretary of State Robert Lansing. Most important, she refused to counsel Wilson to resign, and she made sure that the public did not learn the truth about his health. As a result, the nation had no real president for more than a year. Edith Wilson's experience diminished the role of the first lady by underscoring, in the political memory of Washington, the potential risks of a presidential wife who sought to participate in the substantive aspects of an administration.

Before 1933, none of the first ladies had fully exploited the possibilities inherent in the celebrity status of the institution. Edith Roosevelt had guided public attitudes while Grace Coolidge had fallen in with the rhythms of the age of ballyhoo. Individual elements had been tested—Lou Hoover's radio addresses, Helen Taft's political advice, and Ellen Wilson's support for legislation—yet no one of these women had captured the national imagination and made of the first lady an independent political and cultural force. For the most part, the routine of a president's wife remained "one long procession of tea parties" amid a public that craved to see first ladies "to know how they look and speak and what they wear."

When Eleanor Roosevelt came to the White House, the first lady blossomed as a national celebrity in ways that permanently altered the expectations for presidential wives who followed her. More than any previous first lady, Eleanor Roosevelt cultivated public curiosity in her role as presidential wife.

The regular press conferences with women reporters, which she began upon coming to Washington, were an essential aspect of Eleanor Roosevelt's process of publicizing herself. In a male-dominated world of Washington journalism, Eleanor Roosevelt insisted that only women reporters could attend these sessions. Some of the reporters who attended protected the first lady from tough questions and took potentially embarrassing answers off the record. As members of Mrs. Roosevelt's Press Conference Association, they had as much at stake as she did in maintaining this relationship, and the interdependence of celebrity and media helped her to shape her own public image.

Mrs. Roosevelt also grasped the news opportunities in the position that previous first ladies had not developed. She had no need of a press secretary because she did the job so well herself. She understood, as one reporter put it, that "the American people must make a carnival around their First Lady," and that her travels and appearances would be newsworthy in themselves. Eleanor Roosevelt gave journalists in profusion what a later generation would call "photo opportunities." In her husband's first term, Mrs. Roosevelt became "America's Most Traveled First Lady" as the nation, "unaccustomed to First Ladies darting about, watched her with mingled admiration and alarm."

Eleanor Roosevelt did not limit herself to the passive role of news source. She turned the curiosity about her into a lever that brought offers of writing assignments in newspapers, magazines, and books. She began as editor of a publication, *Babies–Just Babies*, and then wrote an advice column for *Woman's Home Companion* that was called "I Want You to Write to Me." When the magazine ended her column, she began her daily public diary "My Day" in December 1935 for United Features Syndicate.

Popularity gave Eleanor Roosevelt the ability to pursue the causes in which she believed and to find new responsibilities for presidential wives. The good that she did for the unfortunate, the salutary example that she provided on civil rights, and the effectiveness of her place as a gadfly to the New Deal all have been appropriately chronicled. She was less successful in channeling her prodigious energies into constructive and coherent programs of action. Her instinctive response to the people she met as a public figure was to involve them in her life, with resulting distractions that added further complications to an already overburdened schedule. Mrs. Roosevelt believed in work, and as first lady she accomplished much. That the record of her life in the White House added up more to inspiring anecdotes and luminous episodes than to a legacy of programmatic change owed a great deal to her decision to be the celebrity as first lady.

In the weeks following her mastectomy in late 1974, Mrs. Ford received more than fifty thousand cards and messages of good will from the general public—perhaps 10 percent from women who had undergone a similar operation.

The two first ladies who followed Eleanor Roosevelt muted the aspects of the institution that fueled public interest. Bess Truman told friends that she was not "going down in any coal mines," and she gave no interviews, held no press conferences, and limited her public appearances. This retreat from notoriety accorded with Mrs. Truman's own feelings, and it enabled her to play a large role in her husband's decisions in private. Mamie Eisenhower had no ambition to sway her husband on substantive questions, and a chronic illness limited her commitments while in the White House. "She was very much against pushing forward into public view," Dwight Eisenhower said after he left the presidency.

The three years that Jacqueline Kennedy spent as first lady took the institution beyond the status of celebrity and into the even more alluring venue of international stardom. The legacy that Mrs. Kennedy left to her successors was an image of beauty, culture, and good taste that no woman could easily match. A Maine high-school teacher said of Lady Bird Johnson in 1967, "What she suffers from is having had to follow a goddess." The components of Mrs. Kennedy's aura as first lady arose first from her personal allure and her experience in the White House, "the mystical nimbus of tragedy and beauty" that, for many people, she has never lost. Added to it were the dazzling parties and artistic occasions that she and President Kennedy sponsored. Her advocacy of the restoration and renewal of the White House mansion in the style of the early nineteenth-century United States enhanced the impression of gentility and elegance that she chose to convey.

None of the women who followed Mrs. Kennedy has tried to equal her standing as a media figure and public star. Lady Bird Johnson was most successful in finding ways to pursue her own priorities as first lady and in turning the mechanisms of celebrity to her advantage. Coming from a background in the television business and years as an observer of politics, she understood the necessity to provide the press and the electorate with news about what the president's wife did. Mrs. Johnson named Liz Carpenter as her press secretary and had another staff member with responsibility for television appearances. Mrs. Johnson intended to use the fame that surrounded her to achieve substantive policy objectives, and she drew the press into coverage of her campaign between 1965 and 1969 to beautify Washington and the nation.

Celebrity proved less malleable for Patricia Nixon, Betty Ford, and Rosalynn Carter. Mrs. Nixon considered carrying on beautification in 1969, but that and other projects were abandoned in favor of an ill-defined endorsement of "voluntarism." Never comfortable with the personal side of politics and campaigning, Mrs. Nixon preferred to greet tourists in the White House and pursue redecoration of the mansion. That her renovating work rivaled that of Mrs. Kennedy was little known because of personal reticence and the distance of the press from the Nixon presidency. When Watergate broke, the strain of events drove Mrs. Nixon into virtual seclusion by 1974.

Betty Ford was the darling of the celebrity process and also its victim during her White House years. Candor and frankness on social issues made her a favorite of the press and interviewers as a champion of the Equal Rights Amendment and the 1973 Supreme Court decision on abortion. To some extent, media interest in her derived from the contrast between what was felt to be her own cultural tolerance and the more conservative posture of the Ford White House. The sudden onslaught of public attention, combined with her own health problems and the assassination attempts on her husband, tested her emotional resilience and contributed to her dependencies on pills and alcohol that became public knowledge after she left Washington. Despite these difficulties, Mrs. Ford fit rather comfortably into the role of first lady as a symbolic and ceremonial American wife and mother.

Rosalynn Carter wanted more out of being first lady than the institution could give. While she adjusted to the side of her position that operated in public, she sought to be an activist presidential partner and surrogate. This assertion of her influence aroused animosity from reporters and citizens. What was a "Steel Magnolia" doing in Cabinet meetings where men, and perhaps a token woman or two, discussed substance and issues? Mrs. Carter acted in the vein of Eleanor Roosevelt but lacked that earlier first lady's instinct for the right public gesture. She tried to be as constructive as Lady Bird Johnson, only to find that mental health evoked gloom and grimness instead of the warm feelings that natural beauty had summoned. Mrs. Carter thought that a first lady could call the nation to duty. She learned instead that the public wanted diversion rather than moral instruction from the president's wife.

The enduring power of celebrity as a way of defining first ladies revealed itself again in the case of Nancy Reagan. When her expensive lifestyle clashed with her husband's economic policies in 1981–82, her media advisers turned to the instruments of entertainment, including appearances on a situation comedy and self-mockery at the 1982 Gridiron Dinner, to establish her authenticity. From then on Mrs. Reagan received more favorable coverage and the media treated her antidrug campaign with greater seriousness. Until the historical record is available, a judgment on the quality of Mrs. Reagan's effect on the drug problem is premature. The visible side of her program consisted to a large degree of occasions where her fame drew attention to the issue with schoolchildren, parents, and first ladies from other countries in attendance. Still, her publicized involvement with the ouster of Donald T. Regan in 1987 and the ensuing flap over her reliance on astrology in 1988 underscore how much Mrs. Reagan's standing with the public depended on notoriety and celebrity.

Writers on first ladies always confront the question of triviality. Are these women worth studying, and have they had any effect on American history? Their influence on their husbands as wives, mothers, and political partners properly belongs to the field of presidential biography. Historians and political scientists have not devoted much attention to this aspect of the presidency, but there are indications that the balance is shifting, as in the case of recent work on Woodrow Wilson and his wives and the intense fascination with Franklin and Eleanor Roosevelt.

What about the position of first lady itself? To what degree does it represent a legitimate subject of inquiry? Or is it simply a matter of ceremony and a cause of gossip? Ceremony and gossip have surrounded presidential wives throughout American history. The treatment of first ladies as celebrities in this century has only been a way of assessing the place of these women in the politics of the country. The nation is not altogether comfortable with the idea of autonomous, self-reliant women, and it is comforting to have a cultural symbol of femininity who fulfills the stereotypes of what women should be and do.

Being a first lady, then, requires a woman to act, if she would succeed, as a mixture of queen, club woman, and starlet. Subject to unrelenting attention, expected to behave impeccably in every situation, and criticized from some quarter for substantive assertion, the wife of a president has all the perquisites of stardom and the rewards of fame. What she is denied is genuine importance as an individual. Celebrity is a trivializing process, and for first ladies that is the central point of their position. They live on display. While their cage is gilded, their freedom remains severely limited.

Suggestions for Further Reading

There are a number of general histories of first ladies that offer an introduction to the lives and contributions of these women. Betty Boyd Caroli, *First Ladies* (New York: Oxford University Press, 1987) is a scholarly appraisal of all the presidential wives that examines "how the role of First Lady was transformed from ceremonial backdrop to substantive world figure." The book summarizes the state of writing on first ladies before the records in the presidential libraries have become generally available. Paul F. Boller, Jr., *Presidential Wives: An Anecdotal History* (New York: Oxford University Press, 1988) is a distillation based on published sources. Older studies of the first lady include Bess Furman, *White House Profile* (Indianapolis: Bobbs Merrill, 1951), which is a social history of the White House and its occupants; Marianne Means, *The Woman in the White House* (New York: Random House, 1963), a group of sketches of some of the first ladies; and Sol Barzman, *The First Ladies* (New York: Cowles Book Co., 1970). William Seale, *The President's House: A History* (2 vols., Washington: White House Historical Association, 1986) has an abundance of information on the first ladies up through Bess Truman. Elise K. Kirk, *Music at the White House: A History of the American Spirit* (Urbana and Chicago: University of Illinois Press, 1986) is informative on cultural matters.

For Edith Kermit Roosevelt, the only full biography is Sylvia Jukes Morris, *Edith Kermit Roosevelt: Portrait of a First Lady* (New York: Coward, McCann & Geoghegan, 1980). There is a brief autobiographical sketch in Mrs. Theodore Roosevelt, Sr., et al., *Cleared For Strange Ports* (New York: Charles Scribner's Sons, 1927), pp. 5–38. The background of the Roosevelt marriage is treated in Edmund Morris, *The Rise of Theodore Roosevelt* (New York: Coward, McCann & Geoghegan, 1979). Lawrence F. Abbott, ed., *The Letters of Archie Butt* (Garden City, N.Y.: Doubleday, Page & Co., 1924) presents a view of Mrs. Roosevelt from the perspective of her husband's military aide.

Helen Herron Taft, *Recollections of Full Years* (New York: Dodd, Mead & Co., 1914) is a volume of memoirs that came out shortly after the Tafts left the White House. It says more about Mrs. Taft's life in the Philippines than it does about her years as first lady. The standard biography of the president sheds light on his wife as well: Henry F. Pringle, *The Life and Times of William Howard Taft* (2 vols., New York: Farrar and Rinehart, 1939). Ishbel Ross, *An American Family: The Tafts, 1678 1964* (Cleveland: The World Publishing Co., 1964) has further information about Mrs. Taft. Helen Taft would make a very interesting subject for a biography.

Frances Wright Saunders, *Ellen Axson Wilson: First Lady Between Two Worlds* (Chapel Hill, N.C.: University of North Carolina Press, 1985) is a positive assessment of Woodrow Wilson's first wife. Eleanor McAdoo, ed., *The Priceless Gift* (New York: McGraw-Hill, 1962) is a volume of the letters that the Wilsons exchanged during their courtship and marriage. A more extensive record of Ellen Wilson's writing is contained in Arthur S. Link, et al., eds., *The Papers of Woodrow Wilson* (58 vols. to date, Princeton: Princeton University Press, 1966–).

Edith Bolling Wilson, *My Memoir* (Indianapolis: Bobbs Merrill, 1938) provides the romanticized and often inaccurate recollections of the second Mrs. Wilson. The only biography based on the letters that passed between her and the president in 1915 is Tom Shachtman, *Edith & Woodrow: A Presidential Romance* (New York: G.P. Putnam's Sons, 1981). The relevant volumes of the Wilson Papers as published are also helpful. The best treatment of how Mrs. Wilson performed during her husband's illness in 1919–20 is Judith L. Weaver, "Edith Bolling Wilson as First Lady: A Study in the Power of Personality, 1919–1920," *Presidential Studies Quarterly*, 15(Winter 1985): 51–76.

There is no biography to date of Florence Kling Harding, but Francis Russell, *The Shadow of Blooming Grove: Warren G. Harding In His Times* (New York: McGraw-Hill, 1968) has some information about her early life. Ishbel Ross, *Grace Coolidge and Her Era* (New York: Dodd, Mead & Co., 1962) is a sensitive study of Mrs. Coolidge. Mary Randolph, *Presidents and First Ladies* (New York: D. Appleton-Century Co., 1936) offers the insights of Grace Coolidge's social secretary. Helen B. Pryor, *Lou Henry Hoover: Gallant First Lady* (New York: Dodd, Mead & Co., 1969) remains the only biography of an important first lady.

The literature on Eleanor Roosevelt is large and expanding, and any recommendations must be very selective. The best treatment of the Roosevelt marriage and her years in the White House is Joseph P. Lash, *Eleanor and Franklin* (New York: W.W. Norton, 1971). J. William T. Youngs, *Eleanor Roosevelt: A Personal and Public Life* (Boston: Little, Brown, 1985) is a good brief introduction to the most influential first lady of this century. A useful survey of various phases of her career, reflecting the impact of feminist scholarship, is Joan Hoff-Wilson and Marjorie Lightman, eds., *Without Precedent: The Life and Career of Eleanor Roosevelt* (Bloomington, Ind.: Indiana University Press, 1984). Edith Benham Helm, *The Captains and the Kings* (New York: G.P. Putnam's Sons, 1954) is a graceful memoir by Mrs. Roosevelt's social secretary.

Margaret Truman, *Bess W. Truman* (New York: Macmillan Publishing Co., 1986) is a daughter's sensitive treatment of a quiet first lady. Robert H. Ferrell, ed., *Dear Bess: The Letters from Harry to Bess Truman, 1910–1959* (New York: W.W. Norton, 1983) presents the husband's side of the Truman marriage. The record for Mamie Eisenhower is still largely unexplored. Dorothy Brandon, *Mamie Doud Eisenhower* (New York: Charles Scribner's Sons, 1954) is a biography done while she was still in the White House. Lester and Irene David, *Ike and Mamie* (New York: G.P. Putnam's Sons, 1981) is journalistic. Stephen E. Ambrose, *Eisenhower* (2 vols., New York: Simon and Schuster, 1983, 1984), provides relevant information about the Eisenhower marriage and its strains.

The problem regarding Jacqueline Kennedy Onassis is selection from an abundance of polemical and sensational treatments of her life. John H. Davis, *The Bouviers* (New York: Farrar, Straus & Giroux, 1969) is the informed account of a family member. Kitty Kelley, *Jackie Oh!* (Secaucus, N.J.: Lyle Stuart, 1978) is lurid but also has some enlightening material. Mary Van Rensselaer Thayer, *Jacqueline Kennedy: The White House Years* (Boston: Little, Brown, 1967), is based on files that otherwise are not yet open to researchers. Letitia Baldrige, *Of Diamonds and Diplomats* (Boston: Houghton Mifflin Co., 1968) is another memoir from a social secretary.

Lady Bird Johnson, *A White House Diary* (New York: Holt, Rinehart and Winston, 1970) is an unmatched source for a first lady and for the administration of her husband. Liz Carpenter, *Ruffles and Flourishes* (Garden City, N.Y.: Doubleday, 1969, 1970) is both entertaining and informative. Lewis L. Gould, *Lady Bird Johnson and the Environment* (Lawrence, Kans.: University Press of Kansas, 1988) appraises Mrs. Johnson's beautification campaigns in the 1960s and her influence on environmentalism.

Julie Nixon Eisenhower, *Pat Nixon: The Untold Story* (New York: Simon and Schuster, 1986) is a daughter's affectionate study. Lester David, *The Lonely Lady of San Clemente: The Story of Pat Nixon* (New York: Thomas Y. Crowell, 1978) is more detached. Betty Ford, with Chris Chase, *The Times of My Life* (New York: Harper and Row, 1978), is less candid about Mrs. Ford's alcoholism and its effects on her life than is Betty Ford, with Chris Chase, *Betty: A Glad Awakening* (Garden City, New York: Doubleday & Co., 1987). Sheila Rabb Weidenfeld, *First Lady's Lady* (New York: G.P. Putnam's Sons, 1979) is a diary memoir of Mrs. Ford's press secretary that is interesting but must be used cautiously.

Rosalynn Carter, *First Lady From Plains* (Boston: Houghton Mifflin, 1984) is an energetic and valuable memoir of an activist and purposeful first lady. Popular biographies appeared while Mrs. Carter was in the White House, including Dawn Langley Simmons, *Rosalynn Carter: Her Life Story* (New York: Frederick Fell, 1979), and Howard Norton, *Rosalynn* (Plainfield, N.J.: Logos International, 1977).

Nancy Reagan, with Bill Libby, *Nancy* (New York: William Morrow, 1980) is an "as-told-to" autobiography that covers the years before her husband's presidency. Laurence Leamer, *Make-Believe: The Story of Nancy and Ronald Reagan* (New York: Harper & Row, 1983) is critical of the lifestyle of the Reagans. Frances Spatz Leighton, *The Search for the Real Nancy Reagan* (New York: Macmillan Publishing Co., 1987) reflects the skepticism that marked the latter years of the Reagan presidency and Nancy Reagan's role in the White House.

CONTRIBUTORS

LEWIS L. GOULD is Eugene C. Barker Centennial Professor of American History at the University of Texas at Austin.

MARY M. WOLFSKILL is head of the Reference and Reader Section, Manuscript Division, Library of Congress.

DALE C. MAYER is an archivist at the Herbert Hoover Library.

FRANCES M. SEEBER is chief archivist at the Franklin D. Roosevelt Library.

MAURINE H. BEASLEY is professor of journalism at the University of Maryland, College Park.

MARTIN M. TEASLEY is assistant director of the Dwight D. Eisenhower Library.

MARY ANN WATSON is an assistant professor in the department of communication at the University of Michigan, Ann Arbor.

NANCY KEGAN SMITH is an archivist at the Lyndon Baines Johnson Library.

PAUL SCHMIDT is an archivist with the Nixon Presidential Materials Staff.

KAREN M. ROHRER is an archivist at the Gerald R. Ford Library.

FAYE LIND JENSEN is an archivist at the Jimmy Carter Library.

CARL SFERRAZZA ANTHONY has written stories for the *Washington Post* on White House history and also served as Nancy Reagan's speechwriter.

Index

F

G

H

I

J

P

R

S

T

U

V

W